PRAISE FOR . . .

cook
yourself
sexy

"Candice blew me away from the moment she walked in to audition for *Top Chef*. She's amazing!"

—Andy Cohen, host of Bravo's *Watch What Happens: Live* and executive producer of Bravo's *Top Chef*

"Candice has brought sexy back to the dinner table with her newest collection of decadent, bikini-friendly recipes. Get ready for some serious stares when you rock your skinny jeans."

—Frances Largeman-Roth, RD, *New York Times* bestselling author of *The Carb Lovers Diet* and author of *Feed the Belly*

"Candice takes a health-conscious approach toward cooking by combining simple ingredients with classic techniques and incorporating the flavors of her heritage. This combination delivers a fun, fresh, and flavorful variety of dishes."

—Hung Huynh, *Top Chef* winner and executive chef of Catch

"Candice Kumai makes healthy cooking incredibly stylish, sexy, and fun. Her latest book, *Cook Yourself Sexy*, is aptly named, thanks to the mouthwatering recipes that were designed with your healthy, svelte physique in mind."

—Alicia Rewega, editor-in-chief, *Clean Eating* magazine

"The recipes in *Cook Yourself Sexy* reflect Candice Kumai herself: whimsical yet sensible and with just a hint of delicious decadence."

—Chris Santos, executive chef and partner of Beauty & Essex and judge on *Chopped*

"Candice is a rock star. She is both a leader and member of a smart, stylish new generation, and this book is a reflection of that."

—Ari S. Goldberg, CEO of StyleCaster Media Group

cook
yourself
sexy

EASY, DELICIOUS RECIPES FOR THE
HOTTEST, MOST CONFIDENT YOU

Candice Kumai
Photographs by Lauren Volo

RODALE

© 2012 by Candice Kumai

Rodale books may be purchased for business or promotional use or for special sales. For information, please write to: Special Markets Department, Rodale Inc., 733 Third Avenue, New York, NY 10017

Printed in the United States of America Rodale Inc. makes every effort to use acid-free ∞, recycled paper ♻.

Photographs by Lauren Volo
Photograph page 8 by William Waldron

Art direction by Natasha Louise King

Book design by Kara Plikaitis

Library of Congress Cataloging-in-Publication Data is on file with the publisher.

ISBN 978–1–60961–909–1   paperback

Distributed to the trade by Macmillan

2   4   6   8   10   9   7   5   3   1   paperback

RODALE.

We inspire and enable people to improve their lives and the world around them.

rodalebooks.com

♥ Babcia

For the women in my life that
have taught me how to be beautiful.
Strength, Courage, honor & heart.
♥ Baachan, Babcia, Aunt Teruko & Aunt Jadwiga,
thank you for allowing your soul to
touch mine. You forever live thru
my work. You forever live in my heart.
love you always.
♥ Candice ♥

♥ Aunt Jadwiga

Contents

— introduction —

EATING GREAT IS SEXY.

LOOKING GREAT IS SEXY.

So why do you have to choose one or the other?

You don't—no matter what the diet gurus say. You can eat delicious, sexy food and still be the most delicious, sexy you imaginable. You just need to take control of your food—assert yourself in the kitchen and learn to master some elegant, exquisite, exciting recipes.

You see, the keys to looking sexy and cooking sexy are the same: a little dash of smarts and a heaping dollop of self-confidence. If you know your way around the kitchen, you can make foods that will satisfy all of your cravings while also helping you to look and feel your best.

That's what this book aims to help you do. You really can have it all. A trim waist, sleek arms, lean legs, and a butt that turns heads. It's all there; you just don't know it yet. The search for your inner sexy begins here. Sexy isn't in your closet; sexy is in your kitchen.

I felt I needed to write this book because I've become so frustrated with the way we are misled and confused about food. So many of us are tricked into following outdated (I'm talking Tab soda, microwave meals, working out in a neon green leotard thong outdated), unhealthy diet schemes that take the joy out of eating—and don't deliver the shapely, sexy results we were hoping for. Who has ever felt her best while counting calories, starving herself, or eating piles of processed 1989-style "light, fat-free, low-calorie" foods? Not me!

But believe me, that's how I used to eat. I spent my late teens and early twenties modeling, and like a lot of girls in that business, I starved myself; I was a mess of uncertainty and bad habits. If I wanted to look good, I figured I'd have to feel (and eat) poorly. And I was miserable.

But then something happened that changed my life: I went to culinary school. And I discovered that if I took control—cooking healthy, delicious, and yes, sexy foods— I could look good and feel good. It was a revelation!

The confidence I gained has taken me places I never thought I would go, from being cast on the inaugural season of the Emmy Award–winning *Top Chef* to being a repeat guest on shows like *Today*, *Dr. Oz*, and *Access Hollywood*, and becoming a judge on *Iron Chef America*. I've contributed to the #1 *New York Times* bestselling book *Cook Yourself Thin*; authored my first cookbook, *Pretty Delicious*; and written for magazines like *Women's Health*, *Fitness*, *Health*, *Self*, and *Clean Eating.* After extensive research and years of recipe developing, I now know the true definition of clean, wholesome, nutritious food—how to cook it and how to eat it to look and feel happy, healthy, confident, and incredibly sexy every day.

Inspired by my incredible Japanese mother (thanks, Okaasan), I returned to my roots to cook well—and healthy. The recipes in this book are the result. They are specifically designed to be sinfully delicious and guilt free. You'll discover new twists on your favorites, like my Dreamy Butternut Squash Mac 'n' Cheese, and exotic new flavors like Spicy Peanut Soba Noodles. And there's not one, but two chapters dedicated to dessert. (My Port-Soaked Cherry and Dark Chocolate Brownies are a must!)

I'll show you how to get real, use all your senses, balance decadence with moderation, and nourish yourself with natural, unprocessed foods that are rich in FWBs—that's Foods with Benefits! These ingredients deliver a boatload of

nutritional bennies that will keep you naturally gorgeous and sexy from the inside out.

Whether you want to make a major change or just want to adopt some truly awesome habits that will transform your body, get ready to cook yourself sexy. You deserve to feel fabulous every day of your life. I am here to help you whip your fridge, mind, and ass into shape. It just takes a little know-how and a few days (7, to be exact) to jump-start your system and transition to real foods with real benefits. Because sexy isn't in your closet, it's in your kitchen—and your heart.

With love and good taste,

xox, Candice

PS: Have questions? Tweet me @CandiceKumai
For more fabulousness, visit www.CandiceKumai.com.

+ drink more water!

CHAPTER 1

How to Cook Yourself Sexy

What are you wearing when you

feel the sexiest? For some of you, it's a cheeky cocktail dress; for others, it's jeans and a tank top; and yet others will say it's a boyfriend's sweats and T-shirt. Maybe you feel sexiest in nothing at all! Whatever you're wearing, genuine sexiness is all about what's underneath. It's how you carry yourself . . . with confidence! And I know that for many of you, the most intimidating place in your home is the kitchen. Allow me to share the technical skills, secrets, tips, and tricks that will make you feel like a top chef—and cook yourself sexy with amazing nutrients and ingredients that will keep you strong and healthy as well as fine and lovely.

The sexiest bodies don't happen overnight. They aren't in a pill or a shake, and they are definitely not delivered wrapped in cellophane to your doorstep. The sexiest bodies I know belong to people who work for them. They don't eat garbage, and they wholeheartedly commit to some sort of physical activity. Eating well isn't enough to be your best self—ahem, Miss Lazybones, you'll have to get off the couch and move. But I think you'll be surprised at how good it feels, and once you start seeing results in the mirror, you'll never want to stop!

Of course, this book isn't a guide to deprivation or perfection—it's about eating! You can eat absolutely delicious, butter-dripping, crispy fried, pan-seared, chocolate-smeared, indulgent food! This is no gimmicky plan. This is a cookbook that will give you the tools (and the recipes) to get healthy, gain confidence, and become the sexiest you have ever been.

lust versus love: don't settle for a one-night stand on your plate

Ever wake up, roll over, clutch your stomach, and think, "Oh my God, I can't believe I ate all of that last night"? Sister, we've all been there. But there's no need to panic or feel sick to your stomach. Okay, you might feel icky for a little bit. Then take a deep breath and let it go. We need to distinguish food lust from food love.

Listen, I know that lust tends to be an incredible, uncontrollable, impulsive feeling, and sometimes you just have to give in! But if you let your cravings control you, eventually you'll start making bad choices. Never fear: I've created some lust-worthy desserts and treats that should satisfy even your most desperate cravings, like my Grilled Mushroom and Leek Flatbread Pizza (page 130) and Dark Chocolate–Orange Cake (page 222). Otherwise, it's time to start practicing food love.

Love is a beautiful thing, a feeling of bliss! But, like lifelong relationships that blossom out of the best friendships, true love isn't always achieved in a hot minute. Sometimes it takes a little while to see the love that's right in front of your face. Learn to love the right foods, and they'll return your affection—even the ones you weren't so sure about! Try my Kale and Fennel Caesar (page 99) for a delicious, unexpected wow factor that you're sure to fall head over heels for.

adopt a sexy culture as your own

Okinawa, Japan, is considered a "Blue Zone"—meaning Okinawans may have one of the highest life expectancies in the world. In 2000, their life expectancy averaged about 78 years for men and 86 years for women. Okinawans suffer from common diseases at much lower rates than people in Western cultures, perhaps because they focus their efforts on prevention versus battling or treating their health problems. And a healthy, delicious diet is the best preventive medicine!

The more I studied my Japanese ancestry and cuisine, the more I began to realize, this is genius! My grandmother's generation ate as a family. They ate to nurture. They ate until they were 80% full and no more. They did not waste anything. They did not overconsume. They simply ate real, unprocessed and wholesome, foods. Living to nurture one another was a ritual, a family affair, a way of life, and one I have tried to incorporate in my cooking and eating habits. I dine out with friends or host fun, fabulous dinner parties with some of my DIY cocktails. I make food part of the whole experience, not just something to shove in my mouth.

I also grew up in sunny Southern California, where being fit was a way of life. I could wake up and go for a jog, surf, or swim. My friends would meet for a game of tennis, yoga, or a dip in the ocean. A sedentary lifestyle wasn't an option. Plus, there was always a bit of a healthy competition between the ladies. Everyone wanted to make sure that her body was in pristine shape because everyone else's was. Even if you don't live in a warm climate, you can keep a Cali mind-set— where every day is bikini weather!

DO AS CALI GIRLS DO

- Make exercise a priority, and make it fun! Find activities you love, and get your friends to join in. A little competitive jogging– or speed shopping–never hurt anyone. (Well, maybe your wallet.)

- Get outside! Studies show that even 15 or 20 minutes in the sun can help boost your mood. Just be sure to slather on that sunscreen.

- Think bikini. Picture the sun shining on a beautiful beach, and your hot bod in an adorable two-piece. Visualizing your goals can help keep you motivated.

Omegas Do It Better

CONFESSION: I've been having an affair. I'm infatuated with omega-3 fatty acids. You should be, too! The average American adult gets less than 1 gram of omega-3 fatty acids per day. That's it. And that's a huge shame, because omega-3s can do all sorts of amazing things for your body, like:

* Reduce inflammation, which is thought to be the base of many health problems, including heart disease, diabetes, some types of cancers, and arthritis

* Keep your heart and arteries healthy

* Aid in relieving joint pain

* Reduce blood pressure and improve blood pressure response to stress

* Boost your brain, memory, and cognitive function. Emerging research shows that omega-3s help slow cognitive problems such as Alzheimer's disease and age-related cognitive decline

The Best Sources of Omega-3 Fatty Acids

CHIA SEEDS: The wonder seeds! The richest source of omega-3s on Earth, they also have more calcium per serving than milk, twice the potassium of a banana, and three times as much iron as spinach. Chia seeds have a very subtle flavor. Sprinkle on your granola, yogurt, salad, or sandwich.

FLAXSEED: Just ¼ cup of flaxseed contains about 7 grams of omega-3 fatty acids. Evidence shows it may help reduce the risks of heart disease, cancer, stroke, and diabetes.

WALNUTS: The *American Journal of Clinical Nutrition* found that a diet including walnuts helped reduce total and LDL (bad) cholesterol; ¼ cup of walnuts contains 2.8 grams of omega-3 fatty acids.

SALMON: The little fish that started it all. Opt for wild salmon instead of farmed whenever possible. Because of their superior diet, wild salmon are lower in fat and richer in omega-3s than farmed.

SARDINES: A superconcentrated source of omegas. Sardines are also rich in vitamin B_{12} (second only to calf's liver) and protein. Not only is this my favorite fish ever, it's also affordable! So stock up on sardines and save for more stilettos.

WINTER SQUASH: Rich in omega-3s, vitamins A and C, and fiber—that's a win-win-win.

TOFU: A 4-ounce serving of tofu will provide about 0.4 gram of omega-3s. While keeping all soy in moderation, you can still get your omega fix in a hit of tofu.

it's time
to get real

I want you to read the following words out loud: *clean, real, unprocessed, untouched, raw, indulgent, rich*. Doesn't that sound oh so sexy? Maybe you need to read that again, but this time, try using your sultriest voice. Yes!

Now read these words: *chemically processed, lab tested, preservative laden, hormone injected, fillers*. I don't think so. Not even my throatiest, Stifler's mom impression could make those words sound sexy.

I hope it's pretty obvious that real, clean, wholesome eating is the way to go.

It should come as no surprise that millions of people are diagnosed with heart disease, cancer, diabetes, and obesity each year. Perhaps it may have something to do with our diets? As I've mentioned before, many of my Japanese ancestors stuck to a diet virtually untouched by processed foods and junk food fillers. And according to global studies, the Japanese live some of the longest, happiest, leanest lives on the planet. So I'm going to share their secrets and way of life with you.

Don't worry, my American roots still run deep—I love burgers, flatbread pizzas, salads, French fries, and plenty of chocolate! I'm just not going to stuff you until you're so full you can't breathe. I am, however, going to teach you about balance, moderation, and discipline the way that I've learned from my ancestors.

High Standards Apply

Just like men, food can be held to various standards, and yours should be top-notch! You'd never go out with a guy who was rude or careless—why would you ever eat something that made you feel just as bad? Here are a few rules to keep in mind, whether you're grocery shopping or going on a date.

BE PICKY. Look for substance and quality. Don't just give in to any cheap, quick, fake meal. If you're not sure, read the ingredients list carefully (i.e., get a second opinion!).

LESS IS MORE. It's okay to let go and live a little. Go ahead and dabble in a few guilty pleasures. But definitely don't get out of control with the main course. Leave a little room for something later.

CURFEW THAT APPETITE: It's never a good idea to be the last, lurking guest at a party, and the same goes for your plate. Eat too much after 9 p.m. and you might regret it the next morning.

SLOW AND STEADY WINS THE RACE. There's no need to shove your face full of food. (It might be why there was no second date!) If you're looking for a long-term relationship, it's worth taking the time to get to know your food, enjoy the process, and savor every bite.

use all your senses

Before every meal I cook, eat, or judge, on *Iron Chef* or just in my own kitchen, I smell my food. Before I serve anything up to my friends or myself, I take a taste. Before I pull my garlic-rubbed roast chicken or the fresh-baked blueberry spelt cake from the oven, I touch. Whether I'm deep-frying, pan-searing, roasting, grilling, braising, simmering, or boiling, I listen. I love to communicate with my food with more than just my taste buds, and I think it makes me a better cook and a more appreciative eater, and frankly, it's just more fun!

One of the best dates I ever had was with a lovely lad, a bottle of red, and four recipes. A few hours (and some cherries in port wine all over our hands and lips) later, we'd made my Roasted Garlic–Lentil Soup (page 127), Kale and Fennel Caesar (page 99), and Halibut en Papillote (page 169), followed by some amazing Port-Soaked Cherry and Dark Chocolate Brownies (page 229). Needless to say, it was a magical night! Cooking is a language all its own. Learn to communicate with your food, and see if it takes you on a sexy path of your own!

CHAPTER 2

7 Days to Sexy

If you are sick of yo-yo dieting

and deprivation, if you are tired of wasting your hard-earned cash on foods that don't ultimately make you feel good, you're in the right place. Follow me on a journey to the healthiest, hottest you imaginable! In my quest to finally find this place for myself, I've created a mini plan to share my lifestyle with you. It takes just 7 days.

here are the seven basic guidelines of this plan

1   **DRINK MORE WATER.** For the next 7 days, you will be detoxifying, cleansing, and giving your organs a bit of a rest. No highly acidic coffee, no soda or diet soda—only beverages that will heal and nourish your body. Water, sparkling water, tea, and kombucha tea are all allowed. I prefer Good Earth's Sweet & Spicy, Tazo's Green Ginger, or Yogi's DeTox tea. Drink at least *10 cups of water per day* to flush out toxins and negative energy. Think: clean, pure, refreshing. Invest in a reusable water bottle, and carry it with you everywhere.

2   **MEDITATE EACH MORNING.** Start out each morning with a mantra that wipes your slate clean. Focus on a specific purpose (an *ikigai* in Japanese) that will help you get through your day. For example, say to yourself, "Today is going to be an amazing day. I will set my intentions on being positive at work and make sure I take a walk outside at lunch to energize myself." Create a personal morning mantra that works for you. Your morning mantra will give you renewed confidence and help you feel energized and ready for the day's challenges. In a quiet room, sit cross-legged, place your hands on your knees, sit up tall, breathe in, and exhale deeply as you repeat your ikigai.

3   **EAT CLEAN AND REAL WITH FWBS.** That's Foods with Benefits! Aren't you sick of wasting your paychecks on meal plans, protein bars, chalky shakes, and calorie-counting pro-grams? No need, no more! If the produce aisle at the grocery store intimidates you, no worries—I've created a simple chart of FWBs starting on page 240 that makes it easy to stock your kitchen with healthy, real foods. No gimmicks. Take a chance on a new veggie or spice you've never tried before—you'll be surprised at how delish it tastes! Eliminate all processed foods over the next 7 days, and you'll soon see a big difference in the way you look and feel.

4   **PRACTICE THE 75% RULE, AND STAY POSITIVE.** They say that practice makes perfect. But we all live in the real world, and we all make mistakes. That's okay. Over the next 7 days you'll do everything possible to stick to this plan and be your best self. But what if you falter? Just remember the 75% Rule: Every meal should consist of 75% fresh produce. Eat until you are 75% full. Keep 75% of your day active and engaged. If you grab a cupcake for a snack or chow down on a few slices of pizza one night, take a deep breath, focus on staying positive, and say, "Do-over. Tomorrow I will eat clean and real." As you start to practice these sexy new habits, you'll start living a sexier new life without even thinking about it! But for now, do whatever you can to stick to the rules 75% of the time.

5   **BANISH YOUR BAD HABITS.** We all have vices and naughty habits that seem to get us through the bad or stressful times. But for the next 7 days, I challenge you to say no to the following things: no to smoking, no to excess drinking (one glass of vino or champagne is allowed on Friday and Saturday nights), no to late nights out with 5 or fewer hours of sleep. No more deprivation. If you are hungry, eat, but stop when you are 75% full. No overconsuming, no binge eating, no starving, and no drugs of any kind. Sexy is made in the kitchen, not at the bar or the drugstore! As we all know, a miserable, hungover Sunday is not sexy at all.

6   **MOVE TOWARD A SEXIER BOD.** Exercise is proven to be one of the most effective weight-loss aids and stress reducers out there. It's really not hard to do, I promise, and it will make you feel absolutely amazing! All I ask is that you participate in some sort of physical activity for at least 45 minutes each day. It can be a brisk walk, window-shopping with the girls, cleaning out your closet, or maybe even a hot sex session with your guy (challenge him to make it last longer!). I don't care what you do, as long as you move for 45 minutes, every single day. If you are new to exercise or just want to switch things up, I highly recommend that you practice yoga at least three times this week. It's my favorite way to find focus, relieve stress, *and* burn calories. Win-win-win! Jackpot!

7   **GET MORE SLEEP.** Dedicate at least 8 hours to sleep every single night for the next 7 days. Have your husband tend to the kids (blame it on me), postpone any late-night plans, and create a peaceful sanctuary in your bedroom so you can get your ZZZs. Ditch that awful, negative reality show at night, and enjoy fun drama in your dreams instead! Beauty sleep burns more calories, relieves stress, and keeps you happy and energized in the morning. Don't sacrifice sleep—it's the best thing you can do to achieve a more confident, sexier you—and, best of all, it's free.

> "To ensure good health: eat lightly, breathe deeply,
> live moderately, cultivate cheerfulness,
> and maintain an interest in life."
>
> William Londen

the 7 days to sexy eating plan

OKAY, SO WHAT WILL YOU EAT on this amazing weeklong journey? Only the best! Here's a quick rundown of the basic structure of the plan, and on page 16 I've provided a week's worth of sample menus to get you started. And remember: Check out the list of Foods with Benefits on page 240 to load up your pantry with delish, healthy options!

BREAKFAST: If you are hungry, then eat. If you are not, do not consume anything until your body asks for it. Go for a very light protein (like oatmeal or 0% Greek yogurt) and fruit. Keep it light, keep it simple. No meat at breakfast.

LUNCH: Consume 75% greens/vegetables, 15% lean protein, and 10% complex carbs. Fill up on a big green salad with a few slices of lox or sardines in extra-virgin olive oil, or have some roasted root vegetables with a quinoa salad. How about a pita filled with avocados, Fuji apples, spicy hummus, and sprouts? Lunch should be your biggest meal of the day. Go for it!

SNACK: Munch on fresh fruits, vegetables, nuts, and seeds, or opt for a few cups of tea. If you need a pick-me-up, try green tea, chai, Genmaicha green tea, jasmine tea, or lemongrass ginger tea. Switch it up and keep things exciting to help you stay on track. Tea is like internal therapy!

DINNER: Eat a light dinner composed of 75% greens/vegetables and 25% lean protein. Eat until you are 75 to 80% full. You will never again eat until you are "stuffed"! (Of course, Thanksgiving can be an exception to this rule.) Try a hearty bowl of soba noodle or lentil soup or my Kale and Fennel Caesar (page 99).

move over, meat

IN GENERAL, MEAT SHOULD BE limited to an accent on your plate, an accessory to your meal. Cutting down on your meat intake reduces your saturated fat intake, lowers your grocery bill, may help you live longer, and even helps the planet. According to the Johns Hopkins Bloomberg School of Public Health, giving up meat even 1 day a week can reduce consumption of harmful fat by 15%. And a National Cancer Institute study of 500,000 people found that those who ate 4 ounces or more of red meat daily were 30% more likely to have died of any cause during a 10-year period than were those who consumed less. As I've said for years, "Take a backseat, meat!"

reconsider dairy

CALCIUM IS ESSENTIAL FOR GOOD HEALTH, but dairy is not! In clinical studies, dairy has been linked to heart disease, prostate cancer, and irritable bowel syndrome (IBS). You can also get calcium from leafy greens, sesame tahini, and sea vegetables. Green leafy vegetables like kale, chard, collard greens, and spinach are calcium rich. Also check out fortified beverages, such as almond milk and orange juice, and fish, like canned salmon with bones and my favorite—sardines. During the next 7 days, try to eliminate any unnecessary dairy from your diet (0% Greek yogurt an exception). Specifically, you should notice fewer problems with your sinuses, postnasal drip, headaches, and IBS and improvements in energy, weight, and complexion.

Simple Swaps

- Swap regular milk for unsweetened almond milk.

- Swap processed starches for a baked potato, roasted sweet potatoes, or yams or root vegetables galore!

- Swap heavy sauces or bottled dressings for your own fresh, homemade dressings, marinades, and sauces.

- Swap all rice or pasta for quinoa, barley, or farro.

- Replace sugary (and diet—yuck!) soda with seltzer water with a slice of lime or lemon, some raspberries, or a splash of pomegranate or cranberry juice.

- Use all butter and fat/oil sparingly. Don't drown foods in it.

- Swap all heavy meats for lean fish, legumes, and beans.

carbs: separate the good from the bad

"GOOD" CARBS COME FROM WHOLE FOODS loaded with fiber, like fresh vegetables and fruits, whole grains, beans, nuts, and seeds. "Bad" carbs come from processed foods. This includes white flour and white rice (both processed to remove the fiber that's good for us) and refined sugar (the kind that comes from the sugar bowl, soda machine, and candy shop). Try to limit yourself to one serving of nonproduce carbohydrates per day. This can be a whole grain pita or brown rice, quinoa, whole grain pasta, rolled oats, or barley. Choose your carbs wisely, and remember that fiber is your friend!

soy is so-so

ISN'T SOY SUPERHEALTHY, YOU ASK? Well, many of nonfermented soy's nutritional benefits are linked to isoflavones, plant compounds that mimic estrogen. Studies suggest that eating large amounts of isoflavones can reduce fertility in women, trigger early puberty, and disrupt development of fetuses and children. Soy also contains phytic acid, which inhibits the absorption of certain nutrients. Yuck! The good news is that fermented soy has been part of a traditional Japanese diet—that is, some of the healthiest and longest-living people in the world have been eating it—for more than a thousand years. Fermented soy products (like tempeh, soy sauce, and miso) are allowed in limited quantities this week. Nonfermented soy products (including soy milk) are not allowed. Make sure to purchase organic fermented soy whenever possible.

Finally, this weeklong program is your time to become a better you. But that doesn't mean you have to do it all by yourself—ask a friend or your book club to join you! Make it a priority to see friends or family at least one time this week. Involve them in your process, and talk about how you are feeling. Enjoy positive, fun activities, like going to a movie or taking a walk outside in the park. Use your social network to your advantage! Laughter and companionship are key ingredients in a slim and sexy lifestyle.

Some other parting advice to help make this week feel totally restorative: Take a few moments each day to let the sun warm your face and up your vitamin D levels. Buy a cute pair of yoga pants to get you excited for class. Take a nice long shower or bath in the evening. Sip on a cup of fresh mint or chamomile tea before bed. Breathe deeply. Exhale, happy and fulfilled. Note how fantastic your day was and how grateful you are for your purpose in life. You are well on your way to your sexiest self ever!

seven sample menus

USING THE RECIPES PROVIDED, follow this plan—or feel
free to make swaps based on your own preferences.

Monday

BREAKFAST

1 cup tea

1 cup rolled oats and berries

LUNCH

1 cup Roasted Garlic–Lentil
Soup (page 127)

Small Kale and Fennel Caesar
(page 99)

Soda water with lime

DINNER

Warm Fennel and Arugula
Salad (page 140)

Chamomile tea

Tuesday

BREAKFAST

1 cup tea

1 apple, sliced, with
1 tablespoon peanut butter

LUNCH

The Think-Pink Salad
(page 139)

Soda water with orange

DINNER

Hearty Minestrone Soup
(page 80)

Toasted whole wheat pita

Herbal tea

Wednesday

BREAKFAST

1 cup tea

Macerated Fresh Peaches over
Homemade Muesli (page 96)

LUNCH

So Cali Niçoise (page 70)

Soda water with raspberries

DINNER

Homemade Veggie Burger
(page 138) on whole wheat
pita

Detox Apple and Cabbage
Salad (page 100)

Ginger tea

"All things in moderation,
including moderation."

–Julia Child

Thursday

BREAKFAST

1 cup tea

2 Poached Eggs over
Asparagus and Toast
(page 31)

LUNCH

Lox, Caper, and Rocket Salad
(page 72)

DINNER

1 bowl Lime Chicken Soup
(page 78)

Club soda

Friday

BREAKFAST

1 cup tea

Candice's Gone Bananas
Chocolate Oatmeal (page 38)

LUNCH

1 bowl Bridesmaid's Slimming
Soup (page 85)

Toasted whole wheat pita

DINNER

Miso-Glazed Cod with Spicy
Garlic-Braised Baby Bok
Choy (page 110)

Saturday

BREAKFAST

1 cup tea

1 slice Sun-Dried Tomato and
Mushroom Frittata (page 45)

1 slice whole wheat toast

LUNCH

1 bowl Cold Cucumber-
Avocado Soup (page 86)

Kale, Swiss Chard, and
Butternut Squash Salad
(page 102)

DINNER

Orange Miso-Glazed Salmon
over Brown Rice (page 174)

Sunday

BREAKFAST

1 cup tea

Spelt Pancakes with Blueberry
Jam (page 41)

LUNCH

Roasted Tomatoes with Barley
(page 159)

DINNER

Whole Roasted Go-To Chicken
(page 181)

Smashed Fingerling Potatoes
(page 151)

measuring cups

wooden spoon

microplane

mandoline

measuring spoons

tongs

rolling pin

chef's knife

whisk

can opener

fish spatula

vegetable peeler

spatula

serrated knife

paintbrushes

reamer

trigger scooper

wine key

Tools of the Trade

CHAPTER 3

Sexy isn't in your closet—it's in your kitchen! Believe me, your sexiest shape is not hiding under an extra-wide belt or a giant pair of Spanx. Looking and feeling hot is not about dressing 10 pounds thinner, and it's definitely not about eating processed "diet" foods in order to lose those last 10 pounds. Sexy is all about what's underneath. So let's get naked and pare down your kitchen so that you'll always have the right accessories available to dress yourself from within.

TOP PIECES OF EQUIPMENT

TOP PIECES OF EQUIPMENT

1. Chef's knife
2. Tongs
3. Microplane
4. Mandoline
5. Paintbrushes
6. Citrus reamer
7. Vegetable peeler
8. Serrated knife
9. Whisk
10. Spatula
11. Ice cream/trigger scooper
12. Wooden spoon
13. Measuring cups
14. Fish spatula
15. Can opener
16. Wine key
17. Measuring spoons
18. Rolling pin

cook like a pro

NOW THAT YOU'RE ARMED WITH THE RIGHT ingredients, let's talk tools. Ever wonder what you absolutely need in the kitchen? (Probably not that salad spinner you got for Christmas 5 years ago.) The right kitchen tools will fit you like the perfect pair of heels and make you feel like you're rocking a runway as you chop and prep. And you don't have to spend big money on these, either—many of the items below are available at your local grocery store or even from Ikea!

pantry staples and fridge finds

JUST LIKE YOU RELY ON YOUR FAVORITE PAIR OF jeans, you'll reach for these pantry staples every day. They're easy to use and experiment with—you really can't go wrong.

TOP 10 PANTRY STAPLES

1. Extra-virgin olive oil
2. Dijon mustard
3. Sea salt
4. Honey or agave nectar
5. Chicken stock
6. Canned tomatoes, whole, peeled, or diced
7. Cinnamon
8. Balsamic vinegar
9. Worcestershire sauce
10. Peanut butter, organic, natural

TOP 10 FRIDGE FINDS

1. Fresh fruits and veggies
2. Fresh herbs: basil, thyme, oregano, rosemary, etc.
3. Unsweetened almond milk (40 calories per dreamy cup)
4. Fresh onions
5. Butter (irreplaceable—just use in moderation!)
6. Lemons
7. Eggs (my pick: Eggland's Best with more omegas)
8. Goat cheese (especially if you're lactose intolerant, as I am)
9. Soy sauce (I prefer Kikkoman or Tamari) and Sriracha hot sauce
10. Berries

MEGA BONUS!

Once you've stocked your pantry and fridge with the basics, consider a few more items you might want to keep on hand. They're really a bonus for when you feel like kicking things up a notch–you'll be glad you have these at the ready when you need a little extra something after a tough day or to celebrate!

1. Low-fat yogurt
2. Truffle salt
3. Fresh juices: POM Juice, cranberry juice, fresh-squeezed orange juice
4. Champagne (but of course!)
5. Seltzer water
6. Limes
7. Light coconut milk
8. Smoked chipotle chile peppers

parsley

rosemary

fresh berries

arugula

thyme

goat cheese

soy sauce & sriracha

butter

onions

champagne

eggs

worcestershire sauce

oats

barley

sardines

quinoa

sea salt

olive oil

balsamic vinegar

flaxseed

peanut butter

give your palate a makeover

WE ALL HAVE OUR FAVORITE JUNK FOOD and vices, but it's time to get real about what's going in our mouths. Here are healthy swaps to give your taste buds a fashionable—and delicious—update. Once you get a taste of the real stuff, that processed, packaged food might start to look like a pair of acid-washed jeans.

IN	OUT
Almond milk	Milk
Homemade marinara	Jarred sweet marinara sauce
Smoked roasted almonds	Potato chips
Almond milk creamer	Nondairy processed creamer
Homemade salad dressing	Bottled salad dressing
Herbal and green tea	Iced, blended coffee/tea
Organic eggs/eggs	Egg product
Coconut water	Sweetened sports drink
Banana	Processed junk- and sugar-laden bars
Seltzer water	Diet soda
Homemade ice pops	Processed frozen treats
Port wine for dessert	Cheesecake/cake
Sardines	Meat
Arugula/baby spinach for salads	Iceberg lettuce
Toasted almonds or walnuts	Croutons
Dark pure chocolate	Processed candy bars
Organic rolled oats	Sugar-laden cereal
Real wholesome meals	Processed microwavable meals

Of course, there will be those times when you just need to splurge on something truly decadent. How do you indulge without feeling guilty for falling off the wagon? The secret is to know your limits and practice discipline even in the throes of the most outrageous binge. Instead of ordering a big meal for yourself, split a few dishes with your friends or your date. If you're craving a crazy dessert, get others in on the fun—let them do most of the eating, and just go in for a few really big mouthfuls. (Usually that's enough to satisfy a craving anyway.) Remember: Enjoy your food. If you're going all the way, own every bite!

Just like fashion, food can also be so in or so out!

Here are my five favorite indulgences.

1 **CHOCOLATE:** This is quite simply my favorite splurge. Since it's an FWB, I never worry about a li'l nibble here or there! Go for the good stuff: deep, dark, indulgent chocolate. Mmmm.

2 **WINE AND DESSERT WINE:** Opt out of dessert and finish off your night with a glass of port, amaretto, or Limoncello. It's a lovely and satisfying way to get warm and fuzzy, not full, at the end of the night.

3 **BUTTER:** Butter can make anything better—but not when it's smeared on quite possibly everything. Do I cook with butter? Well, duh! Does a Cali girl say "like" every two sentences? Like I said, if you're going to cheat a bit, let it be with the real thing. Go ahead, go with it. Just know when to say when.

4 **FRENCH FRIES:** Now, this is a no-brainer. Who doesn't love French fries? (If you say "not me," I'll call your bluff!) Crispy, salty fries are one of life's greatest pleasures. And my Rosemary-Garlic Fries recipe is waiting for you on page 152.

5 **PASTA:** The no-carb, low-carb diet advice drives me crazy. Carbs are not evil! The trick: Make sure your pasta dish is comprised of 50% or more vegetables, and watch those cream sauces.

cook yourself sexy!

NOW THAT YOU HAVE ALL THE TRICKS of the trade, you're ready to start cooking! Whether you're a newbie in the kitchen or just looking for more great recipes to add to your repertoire, it's time to roll up your sleeves, put on some music, and whip up a healthy, fabulous meal. As you read through the book, you'll no doubt find your own favorites, but here are the recipes every girl should know—they'll become your best friends and never let you down!

MY TOP 10

1. Hearty Minestrone Soup, page 80
2. Marry Me Spaghetti and Meatballs, page 188
3. Kale and Fennel Caesar, page 99
4. Smashed Fingerling Potatoes, page 151
5. Lime Chicken Soup, page 78
6. Cornflake-Chocolate Chip Cookies, page 206
7. Candice's Homemade Marinara Sauce, page 133
8. Whole Roasted Go-To Chicken, page 181
9. Bridesmaid's Slimming Soup, page 85
10. Detox Apple and Cabbage Salad, page 100

"I'm going to be very, very, very happy, and then do everything I have time to do after that."
Abraham Hicks

CHAPTER 4

Brekkie Made Sexy

Rise and shine! Breakfast is the

sunniest part of your morning, no matter what the weather.
You need to nourish yourself but not overstuff yourself. Listen
to your body—it will tell you what it wants and needs. In this
chapter, you will find everything from Poached Eggs over
Asparagus and Toast to nutty Spelt Pancakes with Blueberry
Jam and even crunchy homemade Pumpkin Spice Granola.
Your morning fix doesn't have to be stockpiled with calories,
just flavor!

poached eggs over asparagus and toast

I WAS ONCE TEASED ON *IRON CHEF* by my colleague judge Simon Majumdar
for calling Chef Michael Symon's poached eggs "so sexy." I'll have you know
that poached eggs are the sexiest food in my book. There's nothing quite
like that first slice, when the sultry yolk oozes out from inside the white.
Let the yolks run deep!

FWB: Asparagus, eggs

Makes 2 servings

1 bunch asparagus, woody ends
   trimmed
2 tablespoons distilled white vinegar
1½ teaspoons sea salt, divided
2 eggs
2 slices whole wheat toast
1 tablespoon extra-virgin olive oil
   (optional)
1–2 teaspoons toasted pumpkin
   seeds (optional)
1 teaspoon truffle salt (optional)
½ teaspoon black pepper (optional)

1 Fill a medium saucepan with water and bring to a boil.
   Submerge the asparagus and cook for approximately
   2 minutes, maintaining a bright green color and slight
   crunch. Immediately remove the asparagus from the
   boiling water and shock it in a bowl of ice water.
   Reserve.

2 Fill a medium saucepan about three-quarters full with
   water. Add the vinegar and 1 teaspoon sea salt, and
   bring to a gentle simmer.

3 Individually crack each egg into a small bowl, and slide
   the eggs into the water. Simmer for 4 minutes.

4 Place the toast on 2 plates. Top with the asparagus,
   making an even layer. Using a slotted spoon, lift the
   poached eggs from the water and dab them on a dry
   paper towel to remove excess moisture. Serve over the
   asparagus with the remaining ½ teaspoon sea salt and a
   drizzle of olive oil, the pumpkin seeds, the truffle salt,
   and/or the black pepper, if desired.

PER SERVING: 166 calories, 6 g fat (2 g saturated), 12 g protein,
4 g fiber, 5 g sugars, 527 mg sodium, 18 g carbohydrates

You might notice a lack of black pepper in my recipes. I'm certainly a fan of pepper—for steak,
eggs, and lean ground protein. To me, there's a time and a place for a little extra kick in the pants!

lavender rose petal french toast

MY BEAUTIFUL MOTHER TAUGHT ME that flowers bring joy to any occasion. No words, cards, or hugs can compare to flowers—especially roses, her favorite. With two of my favorite edible flowers in this recipe, you can't go wrong. Start your day with the joy of French toast and flowers!

FWB: Almond milk, cinnamon

Makes 4 servings

LAVENDER ROSE PETAL SUGAR
1 cup sugar
⅛ cup organic dried lavender petals
¼ cup organic dried rose petals

FRENCH TOAST
¾ cup unsweetened almond milk
2 eggs
2 egg whites
¼ teaspoon ground cinnamon
8 slices thick-sliced brioche, challah, or whole grain bread

TO MAKE THE LAVENDER ROSE PETAL SUGAR
Place all the ingredients for the lavender rose petal sugar in a food processor. Pulse until combined.

TO MAKE THE FRENCH TOAST
1 Spray a 10-inch nonstick skillet or griddle with cooking spray. Heat over medium-high heat.

2 Whisk together the almond milk, eggs, egg whites, cinnamon, and lavender rose petal sugar in a shallow dish.

3 Soak a slice of bread in the batter. Place it in the hot skillet.

4 Cook over medium-high heat for approximately 2 to 3 minutes on each side, or until the surface is golden brown and crisp. Watch the heat, as the sugar will burn quickly. Repeat with the remaining slices.

PER SERVING: 424 calories, 6 g fat (2 g saturated), 14 g protein, 6 g fiber, 55 g sugars, 445 mg sodium, 80 g carbohydrates

Freeze leftover French toast and save it for the next morning. Simply nuke in the microwave and crisp up both sides of the French toast in a sauté pan over medium heat. Mmmm.

hangover breakfast burrito

SOMETIMES YOU NEED A KICK IN THE PANTS after a big night out. Here's the ultimate cure for the morning-after blues, packed with amino acids and hangover-fighting ingredients like asparagus, fennel seed, sweet potatoes, and eggs. Feel like yourself again with the real breakfast of champions. Don't forget to drink plenty of water, too.

FWB: Sweet potatoes, asparagus

Makes 2 servings

1 yam or sweet potato, cut into
    ½-inch cubes
2 tablespoons extra-virgin olive oil,
    divided
1 teaspoon sea salt, divided
½ red or yellow onion, chopped
1 cup asparagus pieces, cut on the
    bias
4 eggs, beaten
2 tablespoons fennel seeds
⅛ teaspoon black pepper
2 whole wheat tortillas
1 tablespoon grated Gruyere

1 Preheat the oven to 375°F. Line a baking sheet with aluminum foil.

2 Toss the diced yam with 1 tablespoon olive oil and ½ teaspoon sea salt. Roast for 30 minutes, or until the yam is fork-tender.

3 Meanwhile, heat a skillet with the remaining 1 tablespoon olive oil. Sauté the onion until fragrant, approximately 5 minutes. Add the asparagus and sauté for 2 more minutes.

4 Add the eggs, fennel seeds, pepper, and remaining ½ teaspoon salt to the pan. Cook over medium-low heat until light and fluffy.

5 Lay out 1 tortilla and evenly spread half of the egg mixture down the center. Top with the Gruyere and roasted yams. Fold over one side and roll into a burrito shape. Repeat with the remaining tortilla. Enjoy with a strong cup of coffee!

PER SERVING: 508 calories, 28 g fat (6 g saturated), 21 g protein, 8 g fiber, 9 g sugars, 854 mg sodium, 47 g carbohydrates

pumpkin spice granola

AS I WROTE THE RECIPES FOR THIS BOOK, I realized that I didn't have a signature granola recipe! What the heck? Here's my own take on one of my favorite foods. With the addition of pumpkin and spices like nutmeg, cinnamon, and ginger, this spiced granola will become your new pick-me-up in the a.m.

FWB: Pumpkin, almonds

Makes 6 servings

2 cups rolled oats, preferably organic

½ cup slivered almonds

⅓ cup pepitas (pumpkin seeds)

¼ cup whole flaxseeds

2 tablespoons shredded coconut

⅓ cup pumpkin puree

½ cup maple syrup

1 teaspoon vanilla extract

1 teaspoon cinnamon

½ teaspoon nutmeg

¼ teaspoon ginger

2 tablespoons vegetable oil

1 teaspoon sea salt

⅓ cup dried cranberries

⅓ cup dried cherries

1 Preheat the oven to 325°F. Line a baking sheet with aluminum foil (optional) and coat it with cooking spray.

2 In a large bowl, mix together the oats, almonds, pepitas, flaxseed, coconut, pumpkin puree, maple syrup, vanilla extract, cinnamon, nutmeg, ginger, oil, and sea salt until well combined.

3 Spread the oat mixture evenly over the baking sheet. Bake for approximately 15 minutes. Stir the mixture with a spatula. Return it to the oven and bake for another 15 minutes, or until golden brown and crisp.

4 Once the granola is cool, stir in the cranberries and cherries.

PER SERVING: 404 calories, 17 g fat (3 g saturated), 10 g protein, 9 g fiber, 26 g sugars, 225 mg sodium, 55 g carbohydrates

Not all ovens are created equal, so please watch this recipe carefully. I find that this recipe is cooked best at a low and slow temperature. The granola will crisp up even more after being removed from the oven and cooled properly.

candice's gone bananas chocolate oatmeal

THEY SAY BREAKFAST IS THE MOST IMPORTANT MEAL of the day, so make it count. With hearty organic rolled oats, banana slices, and a touch of natural peanut butter, this yummy recipe will definitely make you go bananas!

FWB: Oats, bananas

Makes 4 servings

4 cups water

2 cups organic rolled oats

2 medium-firm ripe bananas

3 tablespoons natural peanut butter (also amazing with Justin's Chocolate Hazelnut Butter)

1 tablespoon brown sugar

¼ cup chopped dark chocolate

1 Bring the water to a boil in a medium saucepan, stir in the oats, and cook for 3 to 5 minutes. Using a large spoon or a ladle, place the oatmeal into 4 individual bowls.

2 Thinly slice the bananas and place them on top of the oatmeal. Follow by topping each bowl with one-quarter of the peanut butter, brown sugar, and dark chocolate. Mix with a spoon and enjoy!

PER SERVING: 335 calories, 12 g fat (3 g saturated), 11 g protein, 7 g fiber, 13 g sugars, 57 mg sodium, 49 g carbohydrates

open-faced portobello mushroom melts

LOVE HOME FRIES FOR BREAKFAST but worry about eating such a heavy meal? Try this healthy hash stuffed inside a juicy, plump, and flavorful portobello. It's a sexier way to start your morning, without any of the guilt.

FWB: Mushrooms, red bell peppers

Makes 4 servings

POTATO HASH

2 russet (baking) potatoes
1 red bell pepper
½ yellow onion
2 tablespoons canola oil
1 teaspoon sea salt
1 teaspoon paprika

MUSHROOM MELT

4 portobello mushroom caps
1 tablespoon canola oil
2 tablespoons balsamic vinegar
Sea salt to taste
4 slices Gruyère
Sage leaves, chopped

TO MAKE THE HASH

1 Preheat the oven to 375°F. Line a baking sheet with aluminum foil.

2 Chop the potatoes, bell pepper, and onion into approximately ½-inch cubes.

3 Toss the vegetables with 2 tablespoons canola oil and season them with 1 teaspoon salt and the paprika.

4 Bake for 45 minutes, or until the vegetables are tender and browned at the edges.

TO MAKE THE MELT

1 Meanwhile, clean the mushroom caps with a damp paper towel. Scoop out the mushroom gills with a spoon and remove the stems. Toss the mushrooms with 1 tablespoon canola oil and the balsamic vinegar.

2 Place the mushrooms on a baking sheet and bake for 15 minutes at 375°F. When the mushrooms are done and still piping hot, sprinkle with sea salt to taste.

3 Change the oven to the broiler setting. Spoon 2 tablespoons of hash inside each mushroom. Top each with 1 slice of Gruyère, and put them under the broiler for 2 minutes, or until the cheese is melted.

4 Garnish with sage leaves and serve.

PER SERVING: 280 calories, 16 g fat (4 g saturated), 9 g protein, 4 g fiber, 6 g sugars, 464 mg sodium, 28 g carbohydrates

spelt pancakes with blueberry jam

JUST LIKE WITH MEN, I NEED variety in my food! Boring old AP flour just doesn't do it for me anymore. Swap to spelt! Packed with nutrients like manganese, copper, fiber, and protein, spelt flour also adds a nutty, hearty texture to baking and breakfasts.

FWB: Blueberries, spelt

Makes 4 servings

BLUEBERRY JAM

8 cups frozen blueberries

2 cups sugar

¼ cup lime juice

Zest of 2 limes

Rinds of 2 additional limes, reserved
   for thickening

SPELT PANCAKES

2 cups whole spelt flour

1 teaspoon baking soda

1 teaspoon cinnamon

¾ teaspoon sea salt

1¾ cups unsweetened almond milk

1 tablespoon unsalted butter, melted

2 eggs

¼ cup sugar

TO MAKE THE JAM

1 Begin by making the blueberry jam. In a large stockpot over medium heat, combine the blueberries, sugar, lime juice, zest, and lime rinds.

2 Stir to combine and let simmer over medium-low heat, uncovered, for approximately 1½ to 2 hours, or until the jam becomes thick.

3 Using tongs, remove the lime rinds from the jam.

4 Transfer the jam into mason jars and seal them (you should have enough to fill 4 half-pint jars). Store in the refrigerator for up to 1 month.

5 For longer preservation, place the jars in a large stock-pot full of boiling water, making sure each jar is fully submerged with at least 1 inch of water on top. Boil until sealed, approximately 10 minutes. Remove the jars from the water bath and allow the tops to seal; you will hear a "pop" sound from the lid. Store preserved jam in a cool, dry place for up to a year.

TO MAKE THE PANCAKES

1 In a medium bowl, whisk together the spelt flour, baking soda, cinnamon, and sea salt.

2 In a separate bowl, combine the almond milk with the melted butter, eggs, and sugar.

(continued)

3 Form a well in the center of the dry ingredients, and pour the wet ingredients into the dry. Whisk the batter just until the dry ingredients are thoroughly mixed. Let the batter rest for 5 to 10 minutes.

4 Heat a nonstick griddle or heavy skillet (cast iron works best) over medium-high heat. Coat it with cooking spray.

5 When the surface of the pan is hot enough for these lovely pancakes to brown, add ¼ cup of batter at a time. I like to use a turkey baster to keep it nice and clean!

6 Let the pancakes cook on the first side until you see little bubbles begin to form around the edges, approximately 2 to 3 minutes.

7 When the pancakes are just beginning to set on the first side, flip! Let them finish cooking on the second side, about 1 more minute, until golden on each side.

8 Top each spelt pancake with jam and/or your choice of fruit, raw walnuts, maple syrup, or even a dollop of 0% Greek yogurt.

PER SERVING: 362 calories, 8 g fat (3 g saturated), 12 g protein, 5 g fiber, 23 g sugars, 670 mg sodium, 65 g carbohydrates

I love carbs, but I keep it lean by swapping in fresh fruits and veggies. If you're craving carbs, go for it—just cut your serving in half, and add in mouthwatering fruit. Top with macerated peaches (see page 96) or fresh banana slices, blueberries, or strawberries and 0% Greek yogurt.

the antiox
pom-berry parfait

EVERY BREAKFAST SHOULD BE FULL OF FWBs that keep you energized and beautiful. Berries are packed with antioxidants—for vibrant eyes and skin—vitamin C, and a whole lot of tart. This parfait makes a pretty contribution to any brunch or gathering.

FWB: Greek yogurt, pomegranate

Makes 4 parfaits

1 cup 0% Greek yogurt

1 cup fresh berries or pomegranate seeds (or a combination)

¼ cup raw walnuts or almonds

¼ cup agave nectar or honey

In an 8-ounce mason jar or cup, place 2 tablespoons of the Greek yogurt. Top with 2 tablespoons of the fresh berries or pomegranate seeds, followed by 1 tablespoon of the walnuts or almonds. Continue layering your parfait in this order, and top the final layer of walnuts or almonds with 1 tablespoon of agave or honey. Assemble the rest of your parfaits and serve.

PER SERVING: 156 calories, 5 g fat (0.5 g saturated), 6 g protein, 1 g fiber, 20 g sugars, 21 mg sodium, 24 g carbohydrates

sun-dried tomato and mushroom frittata

THE FRITTATA MAY BE THE WORLD'S most underrated BLD! That's "breakfast, lunch, or dinner." This ménage à trois is a tasty trifecta of sun-dried tomatoes, eggs, and mushrooms. All the healthy benefits from the veggies, fresh herbs, and lean protein are sure to make you look and feel fabulous all day long.

FWB: Tomatoes, mushrooms

Makes 6 to 8 servings

1 tablespoon extra-virgin olive oil

1 cup thinly sliced cremini mushrooms

1 leek, white and light green part only, cut lengthwise, rinsed, and thinly sliced in half-moons

2 garlic cloves, finely minced

¾ cup sun-dried tomatoes (dry-packed)

8 eggs, beaten

1 teaspoon sea salt

⅛ teaspoon black pepper

1 tablespoon finely grated Gruyère

2 tablespoons julienned fresh basil (optional)

1 Preheat the oven to 350°F. Lightly grease a round 9-inch or 10-inch pie plate with nonstick cooking spray.

2 Heat the oil in a small sauté pan over medium-low heat. Add the mushrooms and leek to the pan and sauté until just softened, about 8 minutes. Add the garlic and cook until fragrant, about 2 more minutes. Reduce the heat to low and cook until soft and the moisture has evaporated.

3 Place the sautéed vegetables in the pie plate, along with the sun-dried tomatoes. Allow the mixture to cool for about 3 minutes.

4 In a medium bowl, whisk together the eggs, salt, and pepper.

5 Gently pour the egg mixture over the leek, mushrooms, and tomatoes.

6 Place the pie plate on the middle rack of the oven and bake for 35 minutes.

7 Remove the frittata from the oven and cool just ever so slightly. Divide into 6 to 8 servings. Top each with the Gruyère and the fresh basil, if desired. Serve immediately.

PER SERVING: 114 calories, 7 g fat (2 g saturated), 8 g protein, 1 g fiber, 3 g sugars, 342 mg sodium, 6 g carbohydrates

diy dirty mary bar

THE PERFECT WAY TO ENTERTAIN and satisfy your brunch guests without too much hassle? A DIY (that's a "do-it-yourself") bar! Set it up, turn on some music, and let your guests mingle, mix, and help themselves. This recipe makes one large pitcher, so you might want to make a couple in advance, then sit back and enjoy!

FWB: Tomatoes

Makes 4 to 6 servings

3 cups tomato juice
¼ cup olive juice
¼ cup premium vodka
1 teaspoon prepared horseradish
1 tablespoon Worcestershire sauce
¼ cup lime juice
2 shakes chipotle Tabasco sauce

1 In a large pitcher, combine all the ingredients, swirl with a wooden spoon, and add ice as needed. Taste to see if it is to your liking. Like it hot? Add more Tabasco!

2 Serve in chilled, salt-rimmed glasses filled with ice. Top off with a few olives, a twist of freshly ground black pepper, and a cool celery stalk.

Set up the following for your guests:

Glasses	Sea salt (to rim the glasses)
Ice	Black pepper
Tomato juice	Paper straws
Premium vodka	Mini-bar napkins
Olives	Olive brine
Freshly ground black pepper	Chipotle Tabasco sauce
Celery stalks with leaves	Prepared horseradish

PER SERVING: 83 calories, 2 g fat (0 g saturated), 1 g protein, 1 g fiber, 7 g sugars, 780 mg sodium, 9 g carbohydrates

Make Dirty Marias by swapping the vodka for tequila. Rim the glasses with sea salt, and serve them up with some tortilla chips and a lime. *¡Arriba!*

"The key to health lies in
being at peace."
Mahatma Gandhi

CHAPTER 5

Appetizers to Play with Your Senses

Who says you have to skip out

on cocktails and apps to stay sexy, slim, and fabulous? Not me! I have a theory that if you're constantly sharing the love and being the hostess with the mostest, you will get paid back in dividends—or if you're really lucky, in bottles of Champagne. Either way, it's totally worth serving up treats for your friends. Be a lover. Attract more good in your life.

rosemary lemonade

THIS ELEGANT SUMMERTIME FAVE isn't just for the ladies; the rosemary gives it a twist that makes even the toughest dudes ask for a refill. Serve it up over ice in Ginger Sugar–rimmed glasses or mason jars.

sexy cocktails

FWB: Lemon juice, rosemary

Makes 4 to 6 servings

LEMON-ROSEMARY SIMPLE SYRUP

½ cup fresh lemon juice

1½ cups sugar

2 cups water

2 rosemary sprigs, each
approximately 8 inches long

GINGER SUGAR

¼ cup Sugar in the Raw

1 teaspoon ginger powder

FOR THE BAR

Ginger Sugar, to rim the glasses

Mason jars or glasses

Ice cubes

Premium vodka

Chilled seltzer water (optional, if you
want it fizzy!)

Rosemary sprigs, to garnish

TO MAKE THE SYRUP

Begin by making the Lemon-Rosemary Simple Syrup. In a small saucepan, combine the lemon juice, sugar, water, and rosemary sprigs. Simmer gently over low heat, stirring occasionally, until the sugar has completely dissolved. Continue to simmer for another 2 minutes. Set the mixture aside to cool. Discard the rosemary sprigs.

TO MAKE THE GINGER SUGAR

In a small mixing bowl, combine the Sugar in the Raw and ginger powder, mixing well to incorporate. Place the Ginger Sugar on a small plate. Using a clean, wet sponge or paper towel, wet the rims of the glasses and press them into the Ginger Sugar to beautifully rim each glass.

TO SERVE

Fill your Ginger Sugar–rimmed glasses with ice. Add approximately 1 part Lemon-Rosemary Simple Syrup to 2 parts water to 1 part vodka. Finish off with seltzer water to top, if desired, and garnish with a rosemary sprig.

PER SERVING: 148 calories, 0 g fat (0 g saturated), 0 g protein, 0 g fiber, 21 g sugars, 3 mg sodium, 23 g carbohydrates

ooh-là-là love punch

A PRETTY PUNCH MAKES A PARTY feel superfestive. Pour over ice and top off with some pom seeds, lime wheels, or even elderflowers for an elegant touch. This recipe is made in a big batch for the whole group to enjoy, saving time, moolah, and calories!

FWB: Pomegranate

Makes 6 servings

PUNCH
1 lime, thinly sliced into wheels
½ cup pomegranate seeds
3½ cups POM juice
1 cup water
2 tablespoons elderflower cordial
¾ cup premium vodka

FOR THE BAR
Ice cubes
Seltzer water (optional)
More pomegranate seeds (optional)
More lime wheels (optional)
Elderflowers (optional)
Glasses

TO MAKE THE PUNCH

1 In a large pitcher, using a wooden spoon, muddle (gently crush) the lime wheels and pomegranate seeds. Add the POM juice, water, and elderflower cordial. Refrigerate the mixture for at least 15 minutes.

2 Remove the pitcher of the pom mixture from the fridge and add the vodka and ice. Give it a whirl with your spoon just before serving. Add a spritz of seltzer, if desired.

TO SERVE

Pour into glasses and garnish with more pomegranate seeds, more lime wheels, or some elderflowers for an ooh-là-là touch.

PER SERVING: 193 calories, 0 g fat (0 g saturated), 1 g protein, 1 g fiber, 24 g sugars, 20 mg sodium, 26 g carbohydrates

ginger margies

I ONCE DROOLED OVER AN AMAZING ginger margarita at a fabulous NYC establishment—and I knew I could replicate that bad boy at home. The spicy ginger twist and refreshing mint will wow your guests. It's the perfect treat for a sunny spring or summer day.

FWB: Ginger

Makes 6 servings

GINGER SIMPLE SYRUP
¼ cup thinly sliced fresh ginger
1½ cups sugar
1 mint sprig
2 cups water

GINGER SUGAR
¼ cup Sugar in the Raw
1 teaspoon ginger powder

FOR THE BAR
Glasses
Premium tequila
Water
Ginger Sugar, to rim the glasses
Ice
Seltzer water
Fresh mint sprigs, to garnish
Cute paper straws

TO MAKE THE SYRUP

1 In a small saucepan, combine the ginger, sugar, mint sprig, and water. Cook over low heat, stirring until the sugar dissolves. Continue to simmer for an additional 2 minutes.

2 Cool the syrup completely. Discard the boiled ginger and mint sprig. Transfer the Ginger Simple Syrup to a cute jar or squeeze bottle.

TO MAKE THE GINGER SUGAR

In a small mixing bowl, combine the Sugar in the Raw and ginger powder, mixing well to incorporate.

TO SERVE

Moisten the rim of each glass with tequila or water and gently dab into the Ginger Sugar mixture to coat. Fill the sugar-rimmed glasses with ice. To each glass, add approximately 1 part syrup, 2 parts water, 1 part premium tequila, and 1 part fizzy seltzer to top. Whirl with a spoon or cute stir rod and taste-test to perfection. Add as much or as little Ginger Simple Syrup or water as desired. Garnish with a small mint sprig and serve with a cute paper straw. Store remaining Ginger Simple Syrup in the fridge for up to 1 month.

PER SERVING: 309 calories, 0 g fat (0 g saturated), 0 g protein, 0 g fiber, 36 g sugars, 11 mg sodium, 37 g carbohydrates

roasted fig and honey chèvre flatbread

THIS IS ONE OF THE MOST divine recipes—it's also totally easy and customizable! Change it up by adding thinly sliced prosciutto or sautéed pears and blue cheese. Roll out this flatbread paper-thin and bake it just until crisp.

FWB: Figs, arugula

Makes 8 servings

8 fresh figs, halved, tough stems removed

1 tablespoon honey

1 tablespoon + 2 cups balsamic vinegar

1 tablespoon extra-virgin olive oil, divided

1 medium red onion, thinly sliced, preferably on a mandoline

1 pound store-bought pizza dough

Sea salt to taste

4 ounces chèvre (goat cheese)

1 cup arugula

6 slices prosciutto (optional)

1 Preheat the oven to 425°F.

2 Toss the figs in a baking dish or on a baking sheet with the honey and 1 tablespoon of the balsamic vinegar. Roast for 15 to 20 minutes, or until softened. Cool.

3 Heat the remaining 2 cups balsamic vinegar in a small saucepan over medium-high heat until it comes to a gentle boil. Reduce the heat to medium, and simmer until the vinegar is reduced to approximately ¾ cup and has the consistency of maple syrup, about 30 minutes. Cool to room temperature. (The mixture will thicken as it cools.)

4 Heat 2 teaspoons of the olive oil in a large skillet over medium heat. Add the onion and cook, stirring occasionally, until the onion is golden, about 20 minutes.

5 Roll out the pizza dough and place it on a large baking sheet. Bake for about 10 minutes, or until golden brown.

6 Transfer the flatbread to a large platter and brush it with the remaining 1 teaspoon olive oil and a sprinkle of salt. Top with the onions, figs, chèvre, arugula, and prosciutto, if desired. Place back in the oven for about 5 more minutes to crisp up. Remove from the oven, drizzle with the balsamic reduction, and cut into 16 pieces.

PER SERVING: 292 calories, 7 g fat (2 g saturated), 7 g protein, 3 g fiber, 24 g sugars, 298 mg sodium, 51 g carbohydrates

creamy miso dip and crudités

MISO IS FILLED WITH BENNIES like manganese, zinc, and even a bit of fiber. The crunchy veggies make for a supersatisfying, smart snack. Skip the ranch dressing and make miso your new best friend. Miso easy.

FWB: Green onion

Makes 6 servings

½ cup regular mayonnaise

1 tablespoon miso paste, red or white

2 tablespoons thinly sliced green onion, cut on the bias

For the crudités, mix it up! Here are some of my favorite veggies:

Cucumbers, sliced into sticks or rounds

Asparagus spears, ends trimmed

Grape tomatoes

Baby heirloom tomatoes

Endive, leaves detached and separated

Cauliflower, thinly sliced

1 In a small mixing bowl, combine the mayonnaise with the miso paste, whisking well to incorporate.

2 Stir in the green onion.

3 Serve alongside your choice of fresh crudités, and enjoy this dip pre-party or poolside.

4 Save the dip in an airtight container for up to a week.

PER SERVING: 166 calories, 15 g fat (2 g saturated), 2 g protein, 2 g fiber, 3 g sugars, 252 mg sodium, 7 g carbohydrates

homemade apple chutney with gingered toast

EVER SINCE I MOVED FROM CALIFORNIA to New York, I've been obsessed with preserving. Maybe it's those long, cold winters that had me huddled in my apartment for months. Who knows? Whatever the reason, preserving is a great way to keep yummy, healthy fruit around all year long.

FWB: Apples, ginger

Makes 6 servings

CHUTNEY

12 Granny Smith apples, peeled, cored, and chopped into ½-inch cubes (about 12 cups)

1 cup golden raisins

⅓ cup apple cider vinegar

¼ cup light brown sugar

½ teaspoon ground cinnamon

½ teaspoon ground allspice

¼ teaspoon ground nutmeg

2 teaspoons grated fresh ginger

1 teaspoon sea salt, or to taste

2 teaspoons lemon juice

GINGER SUGAR

¼ cup Sugar in the Raw

1 teaspoon ginger powder

GINGERED TOAST

1 tablespoon butter

4 slices whole grain bread, toasted

TO MAKE THE CHUTNEY

1 In a large stockpot, combine all the ingredients for the chutney. Simmer over low heat until the apples appear translucent (approximately 2½ to 3 hours), stirring frequently to ensure nothing sticks to the bottom. Add small amounts of water (1 tablespoon at a time) if the chutney begins to dry out. Once all the apples are fully cooked but not mushy, remove from the heat and cool completely. Transfer to mason jars.

2 For longer preservation: Sterilize the mason jars prior to filling, and follow the manufacturer's instructions to can properly. Immerse the mason jars in a pot of boiling water, ensuring that at least 1 inch of water covers the tops. Boil until sealed, approximately 10 minutes. Remove the jars from the water bath and allow the tops to seal; you will hear a "pop" sound from the lids. Store in a cool, dry place for up to a year.

TO MAKE THE GINGER SUGAR

In a small bowl, combine the sugar and ginger powder.

TO MAKE THE GINGERED TOAST

Spread a thin layer of butter on the toast. (Cut it into 3-inch triangles for mini brunch bites!) Top with Homemade Apple Chutney and a sprinkle of Ginger Sugar.

PER SERVING: 162 calories, 4 g fat (2 g saturated), 4 g protein, 4 g fiber, 17 g sugars, 138 mg sodium, 30 g carbohydrates

smoky red pepper–cannellini dip

WHY NOT GIVE CHICKPEAS A BREAK and trade them in for cannellini beans? They're sweet, bright, and full of fiber. Paired with roasted red peppers, this is an app made in heaven!

FWB: Cannellini beans, red bell peppers

Makes 6 servings

1 (15-ounce) can cannellini beans, drained and rinsed

2 medium roasted red bell peppers

1 tablespoon balsamic vinegar

1 tablespoon lemon juice

1 tablespoon extra virgin olive oil

1 teaspoon smoked paprika

½ teaspoon sea salt, or to taste

Pita bread, cut in wedges and baked (optional)

Crudités of your choice (optional)

1 In a food processor, combine the cannellini beans, roasted red peppers, balsamic vinegar, lemon juice, olive oil, smoked paprika, and sea salt.

2 Pulse until the ingredients form a smooth paste.

3 Transfer the dip to a serving bowl. Plate up with some home-baked pita triangles or crudités, if desired.

PER SERVING: 216 calories, 2 g fat (0 g saturated), 2 g protein, 8 g fiber, 1 g sugars, 213 mg sodium, 8 g carbohydrates

KEEP IT SEXY: Want to make your own roasted red peppers? Turn your gas range's burner on high. Place your washed and dried peppers directly on the grate over the flame. Rotate with tongs until they are evenly charred. Place the roasted peppers in a bowl, and cover them with a plate or plastic wrap for 10 to 15 minutes. Once they have cooled, peel the skin off with a paring knife. Donezo!

Smoked paprika can be hard to find. For an equally smoky alternative, use ¾ teaspoon chipotle chili powder, or 1 teaspoon regular paprika and ¼ teaspoon cayenne pepper.

kimchi for the soul

KIMCHI IS A FOODIE'S DREAM. A popular Korean ingredient, this hot, spicy, garlicky dish is incredible over rice, paired with meat, or just on its own. Warning: If you're planning on making this for a hot date, have mints on hand!

FWB: Napa cabbage, garlic

Makes 8 servings

1 medium head Napa cabbage

2 tablespoons sea salt

1 tablespoon organic granulated sugar

1 whole head garlic, about 10 to 12 cloves

2 tablespoons finely grated fresh ginger, preferably grated on a microplane

¼–½ cup (depending on desired heat) Chinese or Korean chili paste (check your Asian grocer)

¼ cup fish sauce (check your Asian grocer)

¼ cup reduced-sodium soy sauce

¼ cup rice wine vinegar

1 Cut the cabbage in half (lengthwise), then into quarters, and then chop it into 1-inch pieces. In a large mixing bowl, toss the cabbage with the sea salt and sugar. Cover with plastic wrap and place in the refrigerator, allowing the moisture to be drawn out of the cabbage for approximately 3 to 5 hours.

2 In a food processor, combine the garlic, ginger, chili paste, fish sauce, soy sauce, and rice wine vinegar and pulse to combine into a thick paste.

3 Remove the cabbage from the refrigerator and drain the excess water. Combine the chili paste mixture with the cabbage and toss well to coat.

PER SERVING: 59 calories, 2 g fat (0 g saturated), 3 g protein, 1 g fiber, 4 g sugars, 1,534 mg sodium, 8 g carbohydrates

You can store kimchi in well-sealed mason jars and keep it in the fridge for up to a month.

kabocha squash fries
with spicy greek yogurt sriracha

I CAME UP WITH THIS RECIPE as an alternative to my mother's uber-healthy steamed kabocha squash bites. I wanted to Americanize this dish—and the result has become my most-requested appetizer at parties (surpassing even my crab cakes). Serve it up for an instant hit.

FWB: Kabocha squash, Greek yogurt

Makes 4 to 6 servings

KABOCHA SQUASH FRIES

1 (4-pound) kabocha squash, unpeeled, cut lengthwise, seeds removed with a spoon, and cut Into ¼-inch half-moons

2–4 tablespoons extra-virgin olive oil (to taste)

½ teaspoon sea salt, or to taste

SRIRACHA DIPPING SAUCE

¾ cup 0% Greek yogurt

1 teaspoon Sriracha hot sauce (use more or less, depending on desired heat)

¼ teaspoon sea salt (optional)

TO MAKE THE FRIES

1 Preheat the oven to 375°F and line a baking sheet with aluminum foil.

2 In a large mixing bowl, toss the squash and olive oil until well coated. Spread the squash in an even layer across the baking sheet, making sure each piece is touching the surface of the pan, to ensure even browning. Sprinkle with the sea salt.

3 Roast in the oven for approximately 20 minutes, then flip and roast for another 25 minutes.

4 Turn the oven up to 500°F. Continue to bake for another 5 minutes, or until the kabocha squash is golden brown and crispy on both sides.

TO MAKE THE DIPPING SAUCE

In a small bowl, combine the Greek yogurt, Sriracha, and sea salt, if desired. Mix well. Serve alongside the kabocha fries.

PER SERVING: 216 calories, 7 g fat (1 g saturated), 8 g protein, 4 g fiber, 15 g sugars, 201 mg sodium, 33 g carbohydrates

Kabocha can be difficult to cut. I've found that slicing with a ceramic knife rather than a chef's knife spares the arm muscles a bit. Keep it sexy and buff!

smoked tofu and edamame bites*

MY POLISH-AMERICAN UNCLE JOHN loved to tell me a story about how my
Japanese mother was the first person to make him a "meatless sandwich."
This makes even the beefiest of my guy friends beg for more. Trust.

FWB: Edamame, whole wheat

Makes 16 bites

MARINADE

1 tablespoon tomato paste

¾ cup reduced-sodium soy sauce

3 tablespoons honey

1 teaspoon smoked paprika

TOFU

1 block firm tofu, preferably organic,
   halved

1½–2 tablespoons hickory or cedar
   wood chips

EDAMAME HUMMUS

2 cups shelled edamame

1 tablespoon tahini paste

1 tablespoon reduced-sodium
   soy sauce

1 tablespoon lemon juice

8 toasted slices whole wheat bread

TO MAKE THE MARINADE

In a large bowl, combine all ingredients for the marinade.

TO MAKE THE TOFU

1 Wrap the tofu in paper towels and press firmly to remove excess moisture. Place the tofu in the marinade bowl, ensuring that it is completely submerged. Marinate for at least 3 hours, or overnight.

2 Remove the tofu from the marinade and slice each half in half, creating quarters of tofu.

3 Assemble a stovetop smoker according to the manufacturer's directions. Place the wood chips in the base of the smoker. Arrange the tofu on a rack and smoke it over medium heat for 1 hour. Set aside to cool.

TO MAKE THE HUMMUS

Meanwhile, combine all the hummus ingredients in a food processor and blend until smooth.

TO ASSEMBLE THE BITES

1 Slice the smoked tofu into approximately 1- to 1½-inch pieces. Spread 1 tablespoon of edamame hummus on each slice of bread. Lay 2 slices of tofu on 4 slices of the bread, and cover with the remaining 4 slices.

2 Cut the sandwiches into quarters, using a serrated knife to trim off the crusts, if desired.

*Recipe requires a grill or stovetop smoker.

PER SERVING: 148 calories, 3 g fat (0 g saturated), 8 g protein,
2 g fiber, 5 g sugars, 668 mg sodium, 23 g carbohydrates

Home-smoking is much easier than you think! All you need is a stovetop smoker and some wood chips! Check out www.cameronscookware.com. If you don't have a smoker, opt to use sliced baked tofu and a dash of smoked paprika to top.

skinny jean sliders

WHILE SHOOTING A TV SEGMENT WITH Dr. Mehmet Oz, I mentioned that I got my burger fix on by swapping half of the lean protein for caramelized mushrooms and onions. Determined to cut more calories than my last slider recipe, I came up with the Skinny Jean Slider, which Dr. Oz and Chef Todd English both loved. It's up to you whether you want to share the secret!

FWB: Lean ground beef

Makes 8 mini burgers

1 tablespoon canola oil
1½ cups finely chopped cremini mushrooms (about 3 ounces)
1 yellow onion, finely chopped
2 garlic cloves, finely minced
¼ cup finely chopped fresh parsley
1 teaspoon sea salt
¼ teaspoon black pepper
1 pound 96% lean ground beef
8 whole wheat dinner rolls
2 plum tomatoes, thinly sliced
1 avocado, halved, thinly sliced
½ head Bibb lettuce (optional)

1 Heat the canola oil in a medium nonstick skillet over medium heat. Add the mushrooms and onion. Cook, stirring often, until the onion is soft and golden brown, about 15 minutes. Add the garlic and cook for about 4 minutes, just until fragrant. Stir in the parsley, sea salt, and pepper. Turn off the heat and transfer to a medium bowl to cool.

2 Place the lean ground beef in a large bowl, add the cooled mushroom mixture, and gently fold the two together. Divide the ground beef mixture into 8 equal balls, and then gently form each into a semicompact 2½- to 3-inch-thick patty.

3 Heat a nonstick grill or sauté pan over medium-high heat for 2 minutes. Coat the pan with cooking spray and pan-sear the burgers on each side until browned, about 2 minutes per side for medium. Transfer to a plate while you toast the rolls, cut sides down, until golden and etched with grill marks from the pan, about 1 minute. Place each patty on a bun bottom and top with a tomato slice, some avocado, and some Bibb lettuce, if desired. Spread desired condiments such as Dijon mustard, my Agave-Shallot Ketchup on page 152, or BBQ sauce on the other bun half, and top off the slider.

PER SERVING: 210 calories, 9 g fat (2 g saturated), 16 g protein, 4 g fiber, 4 g sugars, 336 mg sodium, 19 g carbohydrates

sweet and salty honey-glazed almonds

I'M OBSESSED WITH SNACKING ON NUTS by the handful! Almonds keep you smart, sharp, and fit. Enjoy this mix at work, as a party snack, or for an energy boost during a weekend hike.

FWB: Almonds, cinnamon

Makes 12 servings

SWEET SPICE MIX
¼ cup Sugar in the Raw
½ teaspoon ground cinnamon
¼ teaspoon ground nutmeg
1 teaspoon sea salt

ALMONDS
3 cups raw almonds
2 tablespoons honey
1 tablespoon Sugar in the Raw
1 tablespoon water

TO MAKE THE SPICE MIX

In a small bowl, combine all the ingredients for the Sweet Spice Mix.

TO MAKE THE ALMONDS

1 Line a full baking sheet with foil or parchment paper.

2 Place the almonds in a medium nonstick sauté pan and roast over low heat for approximately 5 minutes. Turn the heat off.

3 In a microwave-safe bowl or glass measuring cup, combine the honey, sugar, and water. Microwave on high for 2 minutes.* Use caution—the bowl or cup will be extremely hot when you remove it.

4 Carefully pour the honey mixture over the almonds in the pan over low heat, and toss with a rubber spatula to coat.

5 Sprinkle in the Sweet Spice Mix and toss to coat evenly.

6 Spread the almonds in a single layer on the prepared baking sheet. Allow the nuts to cool and set for approximately 10 minutes.

PER SERVING: 240 calories, 18 g fat (1 g saturated), 8 g protein, 4 g fiber, 10 g sugars, 117 mg sodium, 15 g carbohydrates

*NOTE: Microwave times may vary. Test your recipe between 1 minute 45 seconds and 2 minutes.

honeydew and mint wine pops

FROZEN WINE POPS ARE SEXY, SWEET, and refreshing. Blend this version well with fresh mint, honeydew melon, and white wine, and you've got the perfect treat for the next warm afternoon!

FWB: Honeydew, mint

Makes 10 servings

INFUSED SIMPLE SYRUP

1 cup water

1 cup granulated sugar

4 sprigs fresh mint

POPS

½ honeydew melon, peeled and cubed

¾ cup sweet or dry white wine

TO MAKE THE SYRUP

In a small saucepan, combine the water, sugar, and mint sprigs. Simmer gently for 10 minutes. Cool and reserve.

TO MAKE THE POPS

1 In a food processor, blend the honeydew and white wine. Add the syrup and pulse to combine.

2 Pour the mixture into individual ice pop molds, add sticks, and freeze until solid, approximately 6 hours.

PER SERVING: 110 calories, 0 g fat (0 g saturated), 0 g protein, 0 g fiber, 24 g sugars, 10 mg sodium, 25 g carbohydrates

Don't have ice pop molds? No problem. Opt for paper cups lined with plastic wrap, and insert ice pop sticks. Don't have the sticks? Easy. Pour this mix into your ice cube trays, and insert tooth picks for a mini-ice pop treat!

"The beauty of a woman is not
in the clothes she wears, the
figure that she carries, or the
way she combs her hair . . .
but the true beauty in a woman
is reflected in her soul. It is the
caring that she lovingly gives
and the passion that she shows.
The beauty of a woman grows
with the passing years."

Audrey Hepburn

CHAPTER 6

Slimming Soups and Sexier Salads

I'm bringing the slimming soup

and sexy salad back, the way they ought to be—light, fresh, filling, and delicious! Gobs of dressing, condiments, and rancid calorie-laden toppings only add layers to your waist-line. Keep it simple, keep it sexy. These homemade options are sure to fill you up and keep you feeling absolutely fresh!

so cali niçoise

THIS ONE'S FOR CALI: home of the freshest greens, the best avocados, the tannest legs, and a whole lot of sunshine. This recipe is a go-to staple in my house—it's lean, fresh, and lovely. You are what you eat!

FWB: Kidney beans, Tuna

Makes 4 servings

SALAD

2 large eggs (optional)

1 large bunch arugula, washed and dried

½ cup canned kidney beans, rinsed and drained

2 tablespoons capers, whole

¼ cup Niçoise olives, whole

½ red onion, thinly sliced

1 avocado, thinly sliced

1 (5-ounce) can water-packed albacore tuna, drained

VINAIGRETTE

2 tablespoons balsamic vinegar

1 tablespoon Dijon mustard

1 teaspoon agave nectar

2 tablespoons extra-virgin olive oil

½ teaspoon sea salt

TO MAKE THE SALAD

1 If using eggs, in a medium saucepan, cover the eggs with water and bring to a boil over medium-high heat. Cover the pan; turn off the heat, and let sit for 10 minutes. Place the eggs in a large bowl of cold water until they cool completely and can be peeled, about 6 minutes. Peel, thinly slice, and reserve.

2 Divide the arugula among 4 salad bowls. Top each serving with the kidney beans, capers, olives, onion, avocado, tuna, and egg, if using.

TO MAKE THE VINAIGRETTE

In a small bowl, whisk together all the ingredients for the vinaigrette. Drizzle over the salads and serve stylishly!

PER SERVING: 210 calories, 13 g fat (2 g saturated), 11 g protein, 5 g fiber, 4 g sugars, 937 mg sodium, 14 g carbohydrates

KEEP IT SEXY: Cut the salt. Keep your blood pressure low and save yourself a bloated belly by rinsing all of your canned beans and even olives and capers. Be mindful of how much salt you are adding to the dressing as well. Season only when needed.

the get sexy salad

BET YOU A MILLION BUCKS your typical everyday salad won't get you as sexy as this combo. Every main ingredient listed is an FWB—that's a bank-load of bennies to fill you up and slim you down!

FWB: Quinoa, arugula, avocado

Makes 6 servings

2 cups uncooked quinoa

3¼ cups water

1 cup mixed greens, like arugula or mizuna

⅓ pink grapefruit, segmented

½ ripe avocado, thinly sliced

SOY-LIME VINAIGRETTE

2 tablespoons extra-virgin olive oil

2 tablespoons reduced-sodium soy sauce

2 tablespoons lime juice

1 tablespoon balsamic vinaigrette

TO MAKE THE QUINOA

1 Prepare and cook the quinoa according to package directions. If purchased in bulk: In a medium saucepan, add 2 cups quinoa with 3¼ cups water. Cook for approximately 12 minutes, or just until the seeds have soaked up all the water.

2 Set aside the quinoa and cool slightly.

TO MAKE THE SOY-LIME VINAIGRETTE

1 In a large mixing bowl, add the soy-lime vinaigrette ingredients and whisk well to combine.

2 Add the slightly cooled quinoa and toss well to coat with the vinaigrette. Add the grapefruit segments and mixed greens and toss well.

3 To finish, add the avocado slices, top with a squeeze of lime juice or extra soy sauce and dig in!

PER SERVING: 292 calories, 11 g fat (1.5 g saturated), 9 g protein, 5 g fiber, 2 g sugars, 202 mg sodium, 41 g carbohydrates

KEEP IT SEXY: Every ingredient in this salad has health benefits that will keep your body in prime shape! Enjoy with my Orange Miso-Glazed Salmon on page 174 or pair with the Smoked Tofu on page 62 for a completely sexy, healthy meal.

lox, caper, and rocket salad

LOX, AKA SMOKED SALMON, IS LEAN, mean, and megaflavorful. It's loaded with omega-3s, protein, and an arsenal of other benefits. You can't go wrong with this delish fish.

FWB: Arugula, salmon

Makes 4 servings

CAPER-LEMON DRESSING

¼ cup caper brine (from the caper jar)

1 teaspoon dried oregano

2 tablespoons extra-virgin olive oil

1 tablespoon lemon juice

¼ teaspoon sea salt

½ teaspoon honey or agave nectar (optional)

SALAD

4 cups wild arugula

⅓ cup capers

1 cup cannellini beans

¼ cup chèvre (goat cheese), crumbled

12 thin slices lox (wild smoked salmon)

TO MAKE THE DRESSING

In a small bowl, whisk together the caper brine, oregano, olive oil, lemon juice, and sea salt. Add a touch of honey or agave, if desired.

TO MAKE THE SALAD

1 In a large salad bowl, combine the arugula, capers, and cannellini beans. Toss with half of the vinaigrette.

2 Top the salad with the chèvre and lox. Serve additional dressing on the side, if desired.

PER SERVING: 206 calories, 9 g fat (2 g saturated), 20 g protein, 3 g fiber, 1 g sugars, 1,164 mg sodium, 11 g carbohydrates

asian pear salad

DUBBED THE QUEEN OF SALAD MAKING by one of my best friends, Meredith, I'm determined to continue to surprise and inspire my besties, one green plate at a time. This winner has the girls' seal of approval. Bonus: Triple the batch of gingered almonds and save them in an airtight container for the perfect snack!

FWB: Spinach, cranberries

Makes 4 servings

GINGERED ALMONDS
½ cup slivered almonds
2 teaspoons grated fresh ginger
1 tablespoon agave nectar

ALMOST NAUGHTY DRESSING
2 tablespoons agave nectar
2 tablespoons rice wine vinegar
2 teaspoons reduced-sodium soy sauce
1 teaspoon roasted sesame oil

SALAD
3 cups baby spinach
1 Bosc pear, thinly sliced
2 blood oranges, segmented
¼ cup dried cranberries

TO MAKE THE ALMONDS

Preheat the oven to 350°F. Place the slivered almonds on a foil-lined baking sheet. Toss the almonds with the ginger and agave. Bake until golden brown, approximately 15 to 20 minutes. Remove from the oven and cool.

TO MAKE THE DRESSING

In a small mixing bowl, add all the ingredients for the dressing and whisk well to incorporate.

TO MAKE THE SALAD

In a large mixing bowl, combine the baby spinach, pear, oranges, and dried cranberries. Add a light coating of the Almost Naughty Dressing and toss to coat. Finish off with the gingered almonds and serve!

PER SERVING: 218 calories, 8 g fat (1 g saturated), 4 g protein, 6 g fiber, 25 g sugars, 274 mg sodium, 36 g carbohydrates

watermelon and radish salad

LOOKING FOR A SALAD to get fresh with? Packed with nutrients, natural diuretics, and fresh flavors, this salad will leave you feeling satisfied and sexy—without added calories or guilt! Sounds like a sinless choice.

FWB: Radishes, hazelnuts

Makes 6 servings

LEMON VINAIGRETTE
¼ cup lemon juice
2 tablespoons extra-virgin olive oil
1 tablespoon Dijon mustard
1 tablespoon agave nectar
¼ teaspoon sea salt

SALAD
1 small (5-pound) watermelon, or
  ½ large watermelon, rind removed,
  sliced into thin 3-inch triangles
1 bunch radishes, thinly sliced
  (preferably on a mandoline), and
  julienned, radish tops reserved for
  garnish
¾ cup hearts of palm, thinly sliced on
  the bias
½ cup hazelnuts, crushed, to garnish

TO MAKE THE VINAIGRETTE
In a small bowl, whisk together all the ingredients for the vinaigrette.

TO MAKE THE SALAD
In a large salad bowl, combine the watermelon, radishes, and hearts of palm. Toss with half of the vinaigrette. Reserve the other half of the dressing and use more, if desired. Top with the hazelnuts and reserved radish tops.

PER SERVING: 120 calories, 5 g fat (1 g saturated), 2 g protein, 1 g fiber, 15 g sugars, 241 mg sodium, 20 g carbohydrates

Did you know that the green radish top contains more nutrients than the radish itself? With more vitamin C, calcium, and iron, radish tops make you a whole lot smarter, which is the sexiest ingredient of all.

lime chicken soup

INSPIRED BY THE BADASS VIETNAMESE PHO noodle soup (my fave), I began adding lime to chicken noodle soups—I just love that balance of acidity and salt. If you want an extra kick, don't forget to top off those noodles with Sriracha sauce.

FWB: Chicken, carrots

Makes 6 servings

8 cups chicken stock, homemade or store-bought

4 star anise

½ teaspoon chili flakes or 1 dried chile pepper (optional)

2 cups shredded leftover chicken

1 medium carrot, peeled, thinly sliced, and julienned

1 cup sugar snap peas, thinly sliced on the bias

8 ounces rice noodles

Zest and juice of 1 lime

1 tablespoon sea salt, or to taste

Chopped cilantro, to garnish (optional)

Sriracha hot sauce (I use Rooster Sauce) (optional)

1 In a stockpot, bring the stock, star anise, and chili flakes, if using, to a boil.

2 Add the shredded chicken and sliced carrot. Simmer for 10 to 15 minutes.

3 In a medium saucepan over high heat, bring some water to a boil. Blanch the snap peas, shock them in an ice bath, strain, and set them aside.

4 Add the rice noodles and snap peas to the stockpot. Cook for 5 additional minutes.

5 Add the lime zest and juice. Season the soup with the sea salt, as needed.

6 Serve up the noodles in individual bowls. Garnish each bowl of noodles with chopped cilantro, if desired.

7 Squeeze a bit of Sriracha on top, if desired.

PER SERVING: 335 calories, 6 g fat (2 g saturated), 23 g protein, 1 g fiber, 6 g sugars, 504 mg sodium, 46 g carbohydrates

caramelized french onion soup

THIS SWEET, SLOW-COOKED, MELT-IN-YOUR-MOUTH TREAT is one of my favorites. It adds intense flavor to any meal, without megacalories. Cook up a double batch of onions, and save them to top your burgers, pizzas, and sandwiches. They'll keep in an airtight container for up to a week.

FWB: Onions

Makes 4 servings

4 French baguette slices
1 garlic clove, sliced in half
Drizzle + 1 tablespoon extra-virgin olive oil
1 tablespoon sea salt, or to taste
1 tablespoon unsalted butter
3 large yellow onions, thinly sliced
3 teaspoons finely chopped fresh thyme
½ cup dry white wine
6 cups chicken stock
1 tablespoon balsamic vinegar
4 thin slices Gruyère

1 Preheat the oven to 350°F. Line a baking sheet with aluminum foil. To prepare the croutons, arrange the baguette slices in a single layer on the baking sheet. Smear with the garlic clove, drizzle with the olive oil, sprinkle with a pinch of sea salt, and toast in the oven for 6 to 10 minutes, or until golden and crispy.

2 In a heavy stockpot, heat the butter and 1 tablespoon olive oil over medium heat. Add the onions and another pinch of sea salt. Cook, stirring frequently, until the onions are soft and golden brown, about 35 minutes. Stir in the thyme and cook for an additional 5 minutes.

3 Deglaze the pot with the white wine, scraping the bottom to loosen any browned bits. Cook an additional 2 minutes, or until the liquid has reduced by half. Add the chicken stock, bring to a boil, and let simmer for 25 minutes. Finish by seasoning with the balsamic vinegar and the rest of the sea salt.

4 When the soup is finished, switch your oven setting to broil. Arrange ovenproof bowls on a baking sheet. Place a baguette slice in each crock. Divide the soup among the bowls and top each with a single layer of Gruyère.

5 Broil until the cheese melts and the soup begins to bubble, about 8 minutes.

PER SERVING: 360 calories, 17 g fat (8 g saturated), 16 g protein, 3 g fiber, 6 g sugars, 524 mg sodium, 34 g carbohydrates

hearty minestrone soup

WHEN I WAS A LI'L MUNCHKIN, I remember eating minestrone—I still crave that hearty, warm soup—and this homemade version is healthy and satisfying.

FWB: Tomatoes, garlic

Makes 6 servings

2 tablespoons extra-virgin olive oil

1 large yellow onion, finely diced

5 garlic cloves, minced

2 celery stalks, chopped

2 carrots, peeled and chopped

1 leek, halved, cleaned, and finely chopped

1 (15-ounce) can diced tomatoes

8 cups chicken stock

1 (15-ounce) can kidney beans, rinsed and drained (or 2 cups dried and soaked*)

1 (15-ounce) can cannellini beans, rinsed and drained (or 2 cups dried and soaked*)

⅓ cup green beans, trimmed and chopped on the bias

1 cup pasta (penne, mostaccioli, macaroni, or your favorite) (optional—you can skip the pasta to save calories)

1 tablespoon sea salt, or to taste

*If using dried beans, soak in water to cover for at least 3 hours before making your soup.

1 In a large stockpot over medium heat, add the olive oil. Add the onion and cook for about 10 minutes, or until soft and fragrant. Add the garlic, celery, and carrots and gently sweat without coloring the vegetables for about 10 minutes.

2 Add the leek and sauté over medium-low heat for an additional 8 minutes, or until softened.

3 Next, pour in the tomatoes and chicken stock. Bring to a boil, then lower the heat to a simmer and cook for 10 minutes. Add the kidney and cannellini beans, green beans, and pasta and continue to simmer for 20 minutes, or until the beans are soft and the pasta is cooked through. Season to taste with sea salt.

PER SERVING: 281 calories, 8 g fat (2 g saturated), 14 g protein, 7 g fiber, 10 g sugars, 788 mg sodium, 39 g carbohydrates

If you prefer a more robust tomato flavor for your soup, add 1 tablespoon of tomato paste or ¼ cup dry red wine to deglaze the pan after sautéing the leeks. I like to top off my soup with ¼ cup of mizuna greens. They add a fabulous pop of color and even more nutrients!

cannellini bean and leek soup

LOVE BEANS AS MUCH AS I DO? Cannellini beans are an inexpensive and high-quality form of protein that keeps you fuller longer. Use dried beans for the healthiest, tastiest results.

FWB: Garlic, cannellini beans

Makes 6 servings

1 head garlic

2 tablespoons extra-virgin olive oil, divided

4 cups dried or canned cannellini beans (if using canned, add to the soup just 20 minutes prior to finishing)

1 large onion, chopped

4 small carrots, peeled, halved lengthwise, and sliced (about 1¼ cups)

4 tender inner celery stalks with leaves, chopped (about 1¼ cups)

2 leeks, split lengthwise, cleaned, and finely chopped

2 fresh rosemary sprigs

2 cups water

5 cups chicken or vegetable stock, divided

1 teaspoon sea salt, or to taste

1 Preheat the oven to 350°F. Cut the head of garlic in half horizontally, drizzle it with 1 tablespoon of the olive oil, and tent it with aluminum foil. Roast for 40 minutes, or until softened. Peel the cloves into a small bowl and mash them until a paste forms. Set aside.

2 If using dried cannellini beans, rinse them well and place them in a large bowl. Fill it with room-temperature water, just to cover, and allow the beans to soak for 1 hour. Drain and reserve.

3 In a large heavy-bottomed pot over medium heat, warm the remaining 1 tablespoon olive oil and sauté the onion until soft and fragrant, about 10 minutes. Add the carrots and celery and continue to cook, about 5 minutes. Stir in the leeks and cook for an additional 10 minutes, or until soft.

4 Add the beans and rosemary sprigs, cover with the water and 4 cups of the stock, and stir to combine. Bring to a boil, reduce the heat, and simmer, partially covered, until the beans are tender, for a minimum of 45 minutes but up to 1½ hours.

5 To finish, add the roasted garlic cloves and 1 additional cup of stock. Stir to combine and cook until warmed through, about 10 minutes. Season to taste with sea salt. When you are ready to serve, discard the rosemary sprigs and pour the soup into 6 small bowls.

PER SERVING: 400 calories, 7 g fat (1 g saturated), 23 g protein, 13 g fiber, 9 g sugars, 569 mg sodium, 61 g carbohydrates

smoky split pea soup

MY MOM USED TO MAKE THIS divine soup for us after Easter. Leftover ham, anyone? As I began to clean my diet and opt for meatless mains, I realized that I could still get that delightful meaty flavor from smoked paprika. This soup is not only satisfyingly hearty, it's guilt free.

FWB: Potatoes, peas

Makes 6 servings

5 red potatoes

1¼ teaspoons smoked paprika, divided

2 tablespoons extra-virgin olive oil, divided

½ teaspoon sea salt

1 yellow onion, chopped

2 medium carrots, peeled and chopped

5 garlic cloves, minced

2 thyme sprigs

7 cups vegetable stock

1 (16-ounce) bag dried split green peas

1 cup water

Dash of sea salt

1 cup chopped kale (optional)

1 Preheat the oven to 375°F. Wash and properly dry the red potatoes. Cut them in half, then into ½-inch cubes. Place them on a foil-lined baking sheet. Toss with 1 teaspoon of the smoked paprika, 1 tablespoon of the olive oil, and the ½ teaspoon sea salt.

2 Roast the potatoes in the oven for 1 hour. Set them aside. While the potatoes are roasting, begin to chop the onions, carrots, and garlic.

3 In a large stockpot over medium-low heat, add the remaining tablespoon of olive oil. Begin sweating the onion. Cook until soft and fragrant, approximately 10 minutes. Add the thyme sprigs.

4 Add the carrots and garlic to the stockpot and cook until soft and fragrant, about 8 minutes.

5 When the vegetables are ready, add the vegetable stock and split green peas, bring to a boil, and let simmer until the peas are tender, about 1⅓ hours. Add the water and heat through.

6 Right before you are ready to serve, fold in the roasted potatoes. To finish, add the remaining ¼ teaspoon smoked paprika and a dash of sea salt. For an extra-hearty soup, add the chopped kale, if desired, and heat until just wilted.

PER SERVING: 354 calories, 5 g fat (1 g saturated), 16 g protein, 24 g fiber, 6 g sugars, 633 mg sodium, 64 g carbohydrates

bridesmaid's slimming soup

AS A PROFESSIONAL BRIDESMAID (I'VE PROUDLY stood up eight times), I thought it would be highly appropriate to create a soup dedicated solely to this supporting role. Why are there wedding soups and cookies galore but not one dish dedicated to the bridesmaid? What about the girl who holds the wedding together? Stay slim, calm, and satisfied with this delicious soup!

FWB: Barley, kale

Makes 8 servings

1 cup pearl barley
½ cup walnut pieces
2 tablespoons extra-virgin olive oil
1 yellow onion, chopped
2 carrots, peeled and finely chopped
2 celery stalks, finely chopped
1 leek, white and light green part only, cleaned and chopped
2 thyme sprigs
6 cups chicken stock
2 cups finely chopped kale
1 teaspoon sea salt, or to taste

1 Cook the barley according to package directions, until the grains are tender and the water has evaporated. Reserve.

2 In a small skillet, toast the walnuts over medium heat until light golden and fragrant. Cool and reserve.

3 In a deep stockpot, heat the olive oil over medium heat. Sauté the onion until light golden and fragrant. Add the carrots, celery, leek, and thyme sprigs, and sauté until soft and brown at the edges, about 12 minutes. Note: If the vegetables begin to stick to the pot, add chicken stock 2 tablespoons at a time and scrape the browned bits up from the bottom.

4 Add the chicken stock and bring the soup to a simmer.

5 Add the kale and cook until wilted, about 10 minutes.

6 Stir in the cooked barley and walnuts. Finish with the sea salt.

PER SERVING: 267 calories, 11 g fat (1.5 g saturated), 9 g protein, 6 g fiber, 6 g sugars, 485 mg sodium, 34 g carbohydrates

BENEFIT THAT BOD: If you really want to slim down before a wedding or big event, make sure to drink plenty of water and get loads of sleep. It's just as important as what you eat. And try following the 7 Days to Sexy program the week before the big day! Trust me, your ex-boyfriend will drool.

cold cucumber-avocado soup

AVOCADOS ARE HANDS-DOWN MY ABSOLUTE FAVORITE food. They're creamy, rich, and full of health bennies. How does a food get any more perfect? Try this cold, refreshing cucumber soup—it will remind you of summer with every sip!

FWB: Avocados, Greek yogurt

Makes 4 servings

1 English cucumber (seedless), chopped

1 ripe Hass avocado, cubed

¼ large red onion, chopped

2 tablespoons 0% Greek yogurt

1 tablespoon fresh dill

Juice of 1 lime

1½ teaspoons sea salt

1¼ cups cold water

4 fresh dill sprigs, to garnish

1 In a large food processor, combine the cucumber, avocado, red onion, Greek yogurt, dill, lime juice, and sea salt and process for 30 seconds to combine.

2 Stream in the cold water and blend until smooth.

3 Chill for 30 minutes, or serve immediately with a sprig of dill to garnish.

PER SERVING: 75 calories, 5 g fat (1 g saturated), 2 g protein, 3 g fiber, 2 g sugars, 894 mg sodium, 6 g carbohydrates

KEEP IT SEXY: For extra flair, serve this soup in small shot glasses with cute little cucumber cubes on a toothpick, with mini toasts on the side.

Leaving the cucumber skin on gives you extra nutrients and your soup a vibrant green color. Ooh-là-là!

"Goodness is the only investment that never fails."
Henry David Thoreau

CHAPTER 7

In the Raw

Naked. Organic. Real. Raw.

That's what food should be. Many fruits and vegetables are far easier to digest raw rather than cooked, leaving you with more nutrients and fewer added calories and less added fat. Try going raw for just half a day's meals, and watch the pounds fall off. It's a simple commitment, and I bet you'll look and feel like a million bucks!

fresh heirloom tomato salad with chèvre

IF YOU LOVE FRESH CAPRESE SALAD, why not change it up slightly with colorful heirloom tomatoes? With a plate full of vibrant hues, nutrients, and a burst of flavor, you'll impress all your guests with this fun twist on a summertime favorite.

FWB: Arugula, tomatoes

Makes 4 servings

POM VINAIGRETTE

2 tablespoons balsamic vinegar

1 teaspoon Dijon mustard

2 tablespoons POM juice

½ teaspoon sea salt

1 egg yolk

SALAD

3 cups arugula or rocket

2 cups chopped sweet basil

3-4 firm medium heirloom tomatoes, sliced

3 ounces chèvre (goat cheese), cut into medallions

¼ cup pumpkin seeds (pepitas)

TO MAKE THE VINAIGRETTE

In a small bowl, mix the vinegar, mustard, POM juice, and sea salt. Add the egg yolk and whisk until incorporated.

TO MAKE THE SALAD

1 In a medium bowl, mix the arugula, basil, and tomatoes.

2 Drizzle the salad with the dressing and lightly toss to coat. Top with the chèvre medallions. Sprinkle with the pumpkin seeds and enjoy!

PER SERVING: 151 calories, 10 g fat (4 g saturated), 9 g protein, 2 g fiber, 5 g sugars, 419 mg sodium, 9 g carbohydrates

roasted tomatillo salsa and home-baked chili-lime tortilla chips

GROWING UP IN CALIFORNIA, I ENJOYED the best Mexican cuisine, including tomatillos—a sadly underused vegetable in most other states. They're easy to roast, season, and puree. This is a simple way to hit the Mexi-Cali border and bring it back home.

FWB: Garlic, oregano

Makes 6 servings

CHIPS

2 teaspoons chili powder

1 teaspoon sea salt

¼ cup fresh lime juice

¼ cup extra-virgin olive oil

8 (10-inch) flour or whole wheat tortillas

SALSA

1 pound tomatillos, husked

½ red onion, finely chopped

2 garlic cloves

2 chipotle chile peppers (wear plastic gloves when handling)

1 tablespoon chopped fresh cilantro

1 tablespoon chopped fresh oregano

1 teaspoon ground cumin

1 teaspoon sea salt, or to taste

1½ cups water

1 large ear corn, roasted, kernels removed

2 tablespoons lime juice

TO MAKE THE CHIPS

1 Preheat the oven to 350°F and line 2 baking sheets with aluminum foil.

2 In a bowl, mix the chili powder, sea salt, lime juice, and olive oil together until well combined.

3 Place a tortilla on a cutting board, cut it in half, and then cut each half into quarters so you end up with 8 triangles. Repeat with the remaining tortillas. Brush the triangles with the spice mix and place them on 2 rimmed baking sheets so they are just barely touching one another (you may need to toast them in 2 batches).

4 Bake the tortilla triangles until browned and crisp, 12 to 15 minutes, rotating the baking sheet midway through cooking. Remove from the oven and set aside to cool completely before transferring them to a large serving bowl.

TO MAKE THE SALSA

1 Meanwhile, blister the outside of the peeled tomatillos over a gas range or grill, set them aside on a clean work surface to cool slightly, and then slice them into quarters.

2 Place the quartered tomatillos, onion, garlic, and chipotle peppers in a saucepan. Season with the cilantro, oregano, cumin, and sea salt. Pour in the water.

(continued)

3 Bring to a boil over high heat, then reduce the heat to medium-low and simmer until the tomatillos are soft, 10 to 15 minutes.

4 Using a blender, carefully puree the tomatillo mixture and water in batches until smooth.

5 Add the roasted corn kernels and lime juice. Transfer to a serving bowl and serve alongside the home-baked chips. Delish!

PER SERVING: 317 calories, 13 g fat (2 g saturated), 7 g protein, 6 g fiber, 9 g sugars, 912 mg sodium, 45 g carbohydrates

fresh peach salsa

MY LOVE OF SALSA RUNS DEEP, and I enjoy experimenting with new ingredients to keep it fresh. Peaches add a sweet twist to this classic salsa. Whip up this simple recipe to serve with my Home-Baked Chili-Lime Tortilla Chips (page 93) at your next BBQ for a special treat.

FWB: Peaches, tomatoes

Makes 6 servings

5 peaches, pitted and finely chopped

2 plum tomatoes, seeded and finely chopped

½ red onion, finely chopped

⅓ cup finely chopped cilantro

3 tablespoons lime juice

½ teaspoon sea salt

In a large bowl, combine all the ingredients. Toss together and serve with baked chips or crudités.

PER SERVING: 59 calories, 0 g fat (0 g saturated), 2 g protein, 2 g fiber, 11 g sugars, 109 mg sodium, 14 g carbohydrates

KEEP IT SEXY: Host a salsa party! Ask your guests to bring their favorite homemade salsa, pile on the chips, and get dipping. Mix up a batch of Ginger Margies (page 53) to get the recipes swapping and the gossip flowing. Remember, being social is healthy and fabulous!

macerated fresh peaches over homemade muesli

HOMEMADE MUESLI HAS TO BE THE EASIEST, healthiest, yet most indulgent brekkie in a bowl. Add these sweet and tart peaches for the perfect vegan start to your day.

FWB: Peaches, oats, almonds

Makes 8 servings

PEACHES
2 tablespoons sugar
1 cup elderflower liqueur
4 fresh peaches, cut into ½–¾-inch slices

MUESLI
1 cup organic rolled oats (not instant—choose old and rolled; that's the stuff filled with nutrients)
1 cup organic Irish or steel-cut oats
½ cup sweetened shredded coconut
½ cup finely chopped dried apples
½ cup finely chopped dried dates
½ cup golden raisins
½ cup slivered almonds, toasted

TO MAKE THE PEACHES

1 In a large bowl, whisk together the sugar and elderflower liqueur.

2 Place the peaches in the bowl, completely submerging them. Cover. Allow them to macerate (or soften) for at least 3 hours, or overnight.

TO MAKE THE MUESLI

1 In a large mixing bowl or zip-top bag, toss together the oats, coconut, dried apples, dried dates, raisins, and almonds until fully incorporated.

2 Pour the muesli into 8 bowls and serve topped with the macerated peaches. Or throw the muesli ingredients into your cereal bowl, drench it in almond milk and a touch of agave, and enjoy as you would cereal. Yes, you can eat raw oats! And bonus here: They contain more nutrients than instant oats. Word!

PER SERVING: 337 calories, 8 g fat (2.5 g saturated), 8 g protein, 7 g fiber, 38 g sugars, 50 mg sodium, 65 g carbohydrates

Don't have elderflower cordial? Opt for the more traditional Grand Marnier. With a hint of citrus, it's a perfect, fragrant swap.

kale and fennel caesar

DOES YOUR MAN THINK HE'S TOO "manly" for salads? I've heard that a million times! Here's your answer. Loaded with tough kale, crunchy fennel, and protein-packed sardines, this bad boy is even topped with a creamy, hearty Caesar dressing. Trust me, your dude will ask for more (if you're willing to share!).

FWB. Kale, sardines

Makes 4 servings

SALAD

1 bunch Lacinato/Italian kale or
    4 cups kale

1 fennel bulb, trimmed

¼ cup toasted sunflower seeds

1 (3½–4-ounce) can sardines packed
    in olive oil, oil reserved

CAESAR DRESSING

1 egg yolk

1 tablespoon balsamic vinegar

1 tablespoon roasted garlic

1 tablespoon lemon juice

2 tablespoons extra-virgin olive oil

1 tablespoon reserved sardine oil
    from can

¼ teaspoon fresh black pepper

⅛ teaspoon sea salt

TO MAKE THE SALAD

Thinly slice the kale into ribbons. Cut the fennel bulb in half, then thinly slice it into half-moons, preferably on a mandoline.

TO MAKE THE DRESSING

In a large salad bowl, combine the egg yolk, balsamic vinegar, roasted garlic, and lemon juice. Whisk well. Stream in the olive oil and reserved sardine oil, slowly whisking to emulsify the egg and oil. Add pepper and sea salt as needed.*

TO SERVE

Add the kale and fennel to the salad bowl and toss well to coat with the Caesar dressing. Add the sunflower seeds, plate up, and top with the sardines.

PER SERVING: 267 calories, 20 g fat (3 g saturated), 11 g protein, 4 g fiber, 1 g sugars, 256 mg sodium, 15 g carbohydrates

KEEP IT SEXY: Not a fan of sardines? Try anchovies, a salty, classic touch for the perfect Caesar. Or opt out of fish and add ¼ cup freshly grated Parmesan cheese. The cheese will give you that hit of Caesar you need without too many extra calories.

Sardines are mega-salty, so be aware when adding more salt.

detox apple and cabbage salad

I ORIGINALLY WROTE THIS RECIPE WITH the intent of making a healthier version of the fat-laden coleslaw that comes paired with your favorite fried chicken. As I began to experiment, I found that this salad not only has less fat and fewer calories, it has more detoxifying and diuretic ingredients than most of my salads—hence the name. It's a multipurpose, mega-detox treat!

FWB: Cabbage, apples, fennel

Makes 4 servings

DRESSING
2 tablespoons apple cider vinegar
⅛ teaspoon cayenne pepper
⅓ cup 0% Greek yogurt
2 teaspoons agave nectar
1 teaspoon fennel seeds
½ teaspoon sea salt

SALAD
½ head Savoy cabbage
½ head red cabbage
1 Fuji apple
¼ red onion
½ cup roughly chopped walnuts
½ cup golden raisins

TO MAKE THE DRESSING

In a small bowl, add all the ingredients for the dressing. Whisk to combine.

TO MAKE THE SALAD

1 Using a mandoline or sharp knife (for best results, invest in a nice-quality mandoline), thinly slice the cabbages, apple, and red onion to resemble extremely fine confetti. Transfer to a large bowl.

2 Add the walnuts and raisins. Toss gently to combine.

3 Top with the dressing. Using salad tongs, mix until evenly dressed.

PER SERVING: 278 calories, 10 g fat (1 g saturated), 9 g protein, 9 g fiber, 30 g sugars, 371 mg sodium, 44 g carbohydrates

orange and avocado citrus salad

SIMPLE, CLEAN, AND DELICIOUS, THIS IS my go-to "spa cuisine" starter. Whenever I need a moment to escape the heavy grind of NYC and relax, I simply think of Malibu, California —land of sunshine, yoga, and clean eating. This salad will take you there.

FWB. Arugula, orange

Makes 4 servings

SALAD

5 cups wild arugula

1 orange, segmented

1 ripe avocado, thinly sliced

1 small red onion or ½ large red onion, thinly sliced

VINAIGRETTE

Juice of 1 lime

1 tablespoon honey

2 tablespoons extra-virgin olive oil

2 tablespoons 0% Greek yogurt

⅛ teaspoon chili powder (optional, if you like it spicy!)

¼ teaspoon sea salt, or to taste

TO MAKE THE SALAD

Wash and properly dry the arugula. Toss it with the orange, avocado, and red onion.

TO MAKE THE VINAIGRETTE

In a large mixing bowl, combine the lime juice, honey, olive oil, Greek yogurt, chili powder (if desired), and sea salt and whisk well.

TO SERVE

Lightly drizzle the vinaigrette over the salad. Divide among 4 large bowls and serve.

PER SERVING: 172 calories, 12 g fat (2 g saturated), 2 g protein, 4 g fiber, 9 g sugars, 33 mg sodium, 15 g carbohydrates

BENEFIT THAT BOD: Pair this salad with the cold somen noodles from page 109 and hot green Genmai-cha (toasted brown rice green tea) for fabulous spa-worthy cuisine at home.

kale, swiss chard, and butternut squash salad

I WROTE THIS RECIPE AS A simple, immunity-boosting dish to kick colds and nasty flus. With raw butternut squash ribbons, crisp kale, delicate Swiss chard, and an orange vinaigrette, it's simple yet exotic at the same time— kind of like me. Not to mention healthy and delicious (wink, wink!).

FWB: Kale, Swiss chard

Makes 6 servings

ORANGE VINAIGRETTE

1 medium shallot, finely diced

¼ cup pulp-free orange juice

3 tablespoons Dijon mustard

1 tablespoon honey

⅓ cup extra-virgin olive oil

¼ teaspoon sea salt

SALAD

2 medium bunches kale, or about 4 cups chopped

1 medium bunch Swiss or rainbow chard

½ medium butternut squash

½ cup dried cranberries

¼ cup pumpkin seeds

6 ounces fresh chèvre (goat cheese), crumbled

TO MAKE THE VINAIGRETTE

In a small mixing bowl, place all the ingredients for the vinaigrette and whisk to combine.

TO MAKE THE SALAD

1 Clean and thoroughly dry the kale and chard. With a sharp knife, remove the woody stems from the kale. Chop both greens into bite-size pieces.

2 Peel the butternut squash. Halve it lengthwise, remove and discard the seeds, and use a vegetable peeler to slice thin ribbons from the inside of the squash.

3 In a large bowl, combine the greens, squash ribbons, dried cranberries, and pumpkin seeds. Toss with half of the vinaigrette.

4 Transfer the salad to 6 plates. Top with the crumbled chèvre. Serve additional vinaigrette on the side.

PER SERVING: 352 calories, 21 g fat (6 g saturated), 10 g protein, 5 g fiber, 13 g sugars, 423 mg sodium, 36 g carbohydrates

"Learn to make the best of
what you've got."
Natasha Louise King

CHAPTER 8

Asian Persuasion

Asian persuasion? Oh yes, I said

it. But the only fetish here is for clean, delicious food! With a
long, healthy, happy life span on their records, my Japanese
ancestors had it all figured out. I grew up on this cuisine, and
I've done extensive research to refine these recipes for
everyone to enjoy. Allow me to introduce you to the healthy,
and the exotic, Far East.

baachan's miso soup

FOR 92 YEARS (AND COUNTING!), MY *baachan* (Japanese grandmother) has been making this soup. She raised four beautiful daughters through World War II—so she knows a little something about comfort food. My big sis and I sought out Baachan's recipe, which is nothing like your watered-down sushi bar miso. This is hearty, comforting, and as authentic as Japanese food gets.

FWB: Mushrooms, tofu

Makes 6 servings

6 dried shiitake mushrooms

2 large potatoes, cubed

1 cup fish stock (try vegetable stock if not available)

1 piece kombu (a type of seaweed used for stock)*

1 yellow onion, finely chopped

1 carrot, thinly sliced on the bias

1 block of firm tofu, cubed

2 tablespoons dried wakame (smaller seaweed leaves)*

2 tablespoons brown miso paste

1 tablespoon white miso paste

2 tablespoons chopped green onion, to garnish

1 Soak the dried mushrooms in warm water for 10 minutes. Drain and reserve the liquid.

2 Add the potatoes to 4 cups of water in a large pot and bring the water to a boil.

3 Once the potatoes are almost fork-tender, reduce the heat to a low simmer. Add the fish stock, kombu, yellow onion, carrot, firm tofu, and wakame.

4 Add both types of miso paste and mash them into the soup until thoroughly dissolved.

5 Serve garnished with the green onion.

Look for it in Asian specialty stores or online.

PER SERVING: 173 calories, 4 g fat (2 g saturated), 11 g protein, 6 g fiber, 4 g sugars, 463 mg sodium, 32 g carbohydrates

summertime cold somen noodles with ponzu

COLD NOODLES, YOU SAY? WHY YES, it's a Japanese treat! My mom grew up with these noodles as a child in southern Japan and made this dish for us kids on sweltering summer days back in San Diego. Now, I pass along this cool dish to you. Noodles have never been so chill—and refreshing!

FWB: Whole wheat

Makes 4 servings

NOODLES

1 package somen noodles

1 large bowl filled with 1–2 cups ice and water

OPTIONAL SEASONINGS AND TOPPINGS

Ponzu sauce

Rice wine vinegar

Reduced-sodium soy sauce

Hot chili oil

Roasted sesame oil

Katsuobushi (Japanese dried bonito flakes)

Green onions, thinly sliced on the bias

Toasted sesame seeds

Furikake (Japanese Mrs. Dash)

Firm tofu, cubed

Kaiware sprouts (radish sprouts)

TO MAKE THE NOODLES

Cook the somen noodles as directed on the package, strain, and place them in the large bowl filled with ice and water. The noodles should sit nice and pretty in the ice bath.

TO SERVE

1 Serve family-style in the middle of the table. Using tongs or chopsticks, put some noodles into your individual bowls, shaking off any residual water.

2 Add your choice of seasonings and toppings—tofu, ponzu sauce, katsuobushi, sprouts (it's all optional here!)—and enjoy on that hot summer day.

PER SERVING: 225 calories, 2 g fat (0 g saturated), 9 g protein, 3 g fiber, 2 g sugars, 1,137 mg sodium, 43 g carbohydrates

BENEFIT THAT BOD: Somen noodles are a super-healthy—and easy—way to stay slim this summer. The Japanese have been cooking them for centuries. Do as the Japanese do. *Itadakimasu!*

miso-glazed cod with spicy garlic-braised baby bok choy

THIS IS ONE OF THE more popular dishes offered in fancy-pants Japanese restaurants. Now you can make it at home! Low in fat and calories but high in flavor, this simple yet decadent recipe will spice up your taste buds. Pair this dish with sake nigori (unfiltered sake), as well as Japanese beer such as Kirin Ichiban or Asahi, and you've got a fun Aishstyle night in!

FWB: Cod, bok choy

Makes 4 servings

COD

2 tablespoons white or red miso paste

1 tablespoon rice wine vinegar

1 tablespoon roasted sesame oil

1 tablespoon agave nectar

4 (6-ounce) cod fillets, skin on

BABY BOK CHOY

2 garlic cloves, minced

1 tablespoon reduced-sodium soy sauce

2 tablespoons sesame oil

1 tablespoon rice wine vinegar

1 teaspoon agave nectar

½ teaspoon crushed red pepper flakes

Sea salt to taste

5 small heads baby bok choy

1 cup chicken stock

TO MAKE THE COD

1 Preheat the oven to 350°F. Line a baking sheet with parchment paper.

2 To prepare the glaze, whisk together the miso paste, rice wine vinegar, roasted sesame oil, and agave in a large bowl.

3 Baste the cod with the miso glaze and allow it to sit in the refrigerator for 15 minutes. If you're using a whole cod fillet, make sure to portion the fish into 4 pieces. Place the fish, skin side down, on the baking sheet and bake for 20 minutes on the top rack of the oven.

TO MAKE THE BABY BOK CHOY

1 Combine the minced garlic, soy sauce, sesame oil, rice wine vinegar, agave, red pepper flakes, and sea salt in a small bowl. Whisk to incorporate.

2 Cut the baby bok choy into quarters and place in a 13-inch × 9-inch pan. Pour the marinade and chicken stock evenly over the baby bok choy. Cover with aluminum foil and braise on the middle rack of the oven for 10 minutes. Remove the foil and cook for an additional 10 minutes. Remove from the oven, serve alongside the miso-glazed cod, and enjoy.

PER SERVING: 400 calories, 14 g fat (2 g saturated), 46 g protein, 10 g fiber, 18 g sugars, 1,120 mg sodium, 30 g carbohydrates

japanese chicken yakisoba noodles

THIS IS HANDS DOWN ONE OF JAPAN'S favorite street-cart foods. With a simple pan sear for the chicken and a toss of these noodles, it will be just like you're chillin' in Osaka. Don't forget to slurp those noodles up—it's actually polite in Japanese culture. Word.

FWB: Chicken, kale

Makes 6 servings

YAKISOBA

2 tablespoons roasted sesame oil

2 tablespoons Lan Chi black bean chili paste

2 garlic cloves, minced

1 yellow onion, thinly sliced

4 boneless, skinless chicken breasts, cut into 1-inch cubes

½ cup reduced-sodium soy sauce with 1 tablespoon sugar whisked in, divided

2 cups chopped baby kale or finely chopped kale

2 carrots, thinly sliced

8 ounces yakisoba noodles, cooked and drained

OPTIONAL GARNISH

Toasted sesame seeds

Furikake

Gari shoga

Sliced green onion

1 In a large skillet over medium heat, combine the toasted sesame oil and chili paste.

2 Add the garlic and stir-fry for 30 seconds. Add the onion and cook for about 8 more minutes.

3 Add the chicken and ¼ cup of the seasoned soy sauce and stir-fry until the chicken is no longer pink. Remove the chicken from the pan, set aside, and keep warm.

4 In the same pan, sauté the kale and carrots until the kale wilts.

5 Stir in the remaining seasoned soy sauce, then add the cooked noodles and cooked chicken to the pan and toss well to combine all the ingredients.

6 Plate up with tongs and add the sesame seeds, furikake, gari shoga, or sliced green onion, if desired, to top.

PER SERVING: 304 calories, 7 g fat (1 g saturated), 25 g protein, 2 g fiber, 5 g sugars, 1,291 mg sodium, 38 g carbohydrates

Fresh yakisoba noodles can be found in the refrigerated section of Japanese and most Asian markets—absolutely delish!

daikon pickles

I'VE BEEN EATING THESE PICKLES SINCE I was a li'l munchkin! With natural diuretic properties you can actually feel working, daikon radishes are packed with vitamin C, fiber, and potassium. Get ready to meet your new favorite veggie!

FWB: Daikon radish

Makes 12 servings
(approximately 3 cups)

2–2½ pound Daikon radish
¾ cup sugar
1 cup rice wine vinegar
1 cup water
¼ cup salt

1 Peel and slice the daikon in half lengthwise. Thinly slice into half-moons and transfer to a large mixing bowl.

2 In a medium saucepan, combine the sugar, vinegar, water, and salt and bring to a boil. Cook just until the sugar dissolves. Remove from the heat and cool the mixture to room temperature.

3 Pour the sugar mixture over the daikon. After the mixture has completely cooled, cover and place in the refrigerator overnight.

4 Store the pickles in sealed mason jars or an airtight plastic container and save for up to 2 weeks. Enjoy!

PER SERVING: 18 calories, 0 g fat (0 g saturated), 0 g protein, 1 g fiber, 3 g sugars, 249 mg sodium, 4 g carbohydrates

This is the kind of sexy side dish you can consume lots of! Packed with natural detoxifying properties, these pickles can be consumed over brown rice, thrown into soups and salads, or eaten on their own as a snack.

pho and champagne in bed

WHEN PEOPLE ASK ME WHAT MY dream date is, I politely reply, "Champagne and pho . . . in bed!" Whether you're snuggled up with your sweetie, on your own in comfy pajamas, or with some girlfriends, this recipe is a megahit (sure, even at the good ol' dinner table). Enjoy one of my all-time favorites!

FWB: Chicken

Makes 6 servings

PHO SOUP
1 small yellow onion, unpeeled

5 garlic cloves, unpeeled

1 whole (4–5-pound) chicken, innards removed

2 teaspoons sea salt

8 star anise

2 cinnamon sticks

1 lemongrass shoot, sliced into 4-inch strips, or 1 teaspoon lemon zest

2 tablespoons fish sauce, or to taste

¼ cup reduced-sodium soy sauce

1 teaspoon sea salt, or to taste

1 (14-ounce) box flat rice noodles (found at the Asian grocer)

4 ounces bean sprouts (optional)

4 green onions, sliced (optional)

¾ cup chopped cilantro (optional)

OPTIONAL GARNISH
Lime wedges

Fresh mint

Fresh basil

Sriracha hot sauce

1 Preheat the oven to 350°F. Roast the onion and garlic on a small baking sheet until their skins turn a crisp, golden brown. Cool and peel.

2 Wash and clean the whole chicken, then pat it dry. Lightly salt the chicken inside the cavity and out, using the 2 teaspoons of sea salt, and then place it in a medium pot. Add enough room-temperature water to cover the bird (about 10 to 15 cups), along with the star anise, cinnamon, and lemongrass.

3 Simmer lightly over medium-high heat for 1½ to 2 hours, or until the chicken reaches an internal temperature of 165°F. Remove the chicken from the pot and set aside. Save the broth and keep it at a simmer.

4 Add the roasted onion and garlic, fish sauce, and soy sauce to the broth. Simmer for another 2 to 3 hours. Meanwhile, remove the cooled chicken from the bone and shred it on a cutting board. Add the bones back into the broth while it simmers for the remaining cooking time for more intense flavor. Season to taste, using approximately 1 teaspoon of salt.

5 In an additional large pot, add water and boil the rice noodles as directed on the package.

6 To plate: Pop that Champagne and toast to the best soup you've ever made. Place the noodles into 6 individual

(continued)

bowls and top with your choice of bean sprouts, green onions, and cilantro, and the shredded chicken. Ladle hot broth on top of each bowl to create a delish soup. Garnish with your choice of lime wedges, fresh mint or basil, and lots of Sriracha!

PER SERVING: 301 calories, 1 g fat (0 g saturated), 10 g protein, 1 g fiber, 2 g sugars, 1,112 mg sodium, 62 g carbohydrates

To save time in steps 2 and 3, use premade chicken stock and a cooked rotisserie chicken. Pair with your favorite Champagne or sparkling wine.

vegetable gyoza
with orange ponzu sauce

MY MOM MAKES KILLER GYOZA THAT everyone devours—from the Polish side of my family to friends far and wide. I've learned the best things in life from my mom's influence, and this recipe is no exception. Here's my lighter, vegan version of this bad boy.

FWB: Cabbage, mushrooms

Makes 40 gyoza

GYOZA

2 cups finely chopped cabbage

4 cups finely chopped shiitake mushrooms, stems removed

½ yellow onion, finely chopped

3 green onions, finely chopped

4 garlic cloves, minced

2 teaspoons minced fresh ginger, or 1 teaspoon ginger powder

1 tablespoon roasted sesame seeds

¼ cup reduced-sodium soy sauce

2 tablespoons roasted sesame oil

1 tablespoon sugar

1 cup panko breadcrumbs

1 package (approximately 40–50) gyoza or wonton wrappers

1 tablespoon canola oil + additional, if needed

ORANGE PONZU SAUCE

¼ cup reduced-sodium soy sauce

3 tablespoons rice wine vinegar

1 teaspoon freshly grated orange zest

1 teaspoon sugar (optional)

TO MAKE THE GYOZA

1 In a large mixing bowl, add the cabbage, shiitake mushrooms, onions, garlic, ginger, and sesame seeds. Toss well to combine. Mix the soy sauce, roasted sesame oil, and sugar together and add all at once. Stir until well combined. Fold in the panko.*

2 To assemble the gyoza, dust your work surface with some flour. Place a small bowl of water next to your work area. Set out 10 wrappers on the floured area and place 2 teaspoons of gyoza filling in the center of each.

3 Use your fingers to moisten the edges of 1 wrapper with water, and then fold the wrapper over the filling (as if you were making a turnover) and press the edges together. Use your index finger and thumb to pinch the edges so that they have a cute ruffled look (like the edge of a piecrust). Set aside and repeat with the rest of the filling and wrappers.

4 To cook the gyoza, heat the oil in a large skillet over medium heat for 1 to 2 minutes. Place 10 gyoza or so in the skillet with a bit of elbow room in between. Cover with a lid. Cook for approximately 3 to 4 minutes on one side, or until golden brown.

*NOTE: Do not let this filling sit for longer than 30 minutes, as the cabbage and other vegetables will begin to release their liquids, and you will have soggy gyoza!

(continued)

5 When the gyoza are finished, turn off the heat, pour the excess oil from the pan into a bowl, and set it aside for the next batch. Remove the lid and carefully place a large plate over the skillet (the plate should be larger than the skillet). Flip the pan over—the gyoza should effortlessly fall from the pan to the plate, revealing their gorgeous, golden brown skins. Gyoza taste best when hot, so serve immediately with the Orange Ponzu Sauce as you cook up the next batch. Add more oil as needed for each batch. Wipe out the skillet between batches, if necessary.

TO MAKE THE ORANGE PONZU SAUCE

While the gyoza cook, make the Orange Ponzu Sauce. Whisk the soy sauce and rice wine vinegar together in a small dish. Add the orange zest and sugar, if desired. Serve alongside the gyoza, as a dipping sauce

PER SERVING: 47 calories, 1 g fat (0 g saturated), 1 g protein, 1 g fiber, 1 g sugars, 162 mg sodium, 7 g carbohydrates

KEEP IT SEXY: Opt for homemade gyoza skins (sans eggs), and you'll serve up a healthy, nutritious vegan dream.

nori hand rolls

FRESH SUSHI WAS A STAPLE in our household, and of course my mom made the absolute best. Ask her what her quick go-to recipe is and she will say, "Sushi. It's so easy!" Mom, you are talented at everything you do. But for the rest of us, here's a simple sushi recipe that won't leave you frustrated. Roll away!

FWB: Brown rice

Makes 4 to 6 servings

10-12 sheets toasted nori (seaweed)
2-3 cups cooked brown rice

OPTIONAL FILLERS
1 ripe avocado, thinly sliced
Fresh basil, stems removed
Cucumber, thinly sliced lengthwise
Fresh cilantro sprigs
Carrots, thinly sliced
Japanese kaiware sprouts
Japanese umeboshi plums, seeds discarded
Daikon Pickles (page 112)

OPTIONAL PROTEINS
Imitation crabmeat pieces or sticks
Smoked salmon, thinly sliced
Smoked tofu, thinly sliced (see page 62)

OPTIONAL SEASONINGS
Furikake (Japanese Mrs. Dash)
Toasted sesame seeds
Togarashi
Sriracha hot sauce

Reduced-sodium soy sauce, for dipping
Ponzu sauce, for dipping

1 Using kitchen shears, cut the nori in half. You should have 20 to 24 half sheets. Have ready a small bowl of room-temperature water.

2 Place the nori half vertically in front of you on a clean surface.

3 Place approximately ¼ cup of brown rice diagonally on the bottom left corner of a nori sheet. Top with your choice of fillers, proteins, and seasonings. Tightly roll the nori into a cone shape around the filling and seal the edge of the nori with a dab of water.

4 Dip in your choice of sauces or just enjoy as is!

PER SERVING: 269 calories, 6 g fat (1 g saturated), 12 g protein, 6 g fiber, 5 g sugars, 1,300 mg sodium, 40 g carbohydrates

spicy peanut soba noodles

THIS RECIPE IS A FAVORITE WITH my *ohana* in Hawaii. With fresh, sweet red bell peppers; Japanese eggplant; and a simple, yet exotic, rice wine vinaigrette, you can't go wrong. Soba noodles are packed with protein and fiber, and most varieties are gluten free. Try something new and exciting!

FWB: Soba, eggplant

Makes 8 servings

SOBA NOODLES

1 cup quartered and thinly sliced Japanese eggplant

1 tablespoon roasted sesame oil

1 tablespoon reduced-sodium soy sauce

1 (8-ounce) package soba noodles

1 red bell pepper, seeded and thinly sliced

1 cup arugula or mizuna greens

2 tablespoons crushed peanuts (optional)

2 tablespoons Thai basil or regular basil (optional)

VINAIGRETTE

2 tablespoons natural peanut butter

1 teaspoon reduced-sodium soy sauce

2 tablespoons roasted sesame oil

2 tablespoons rice wine vinegar

1 teaspoon Sriracha hot sauce

1 teaspoon honey

TO MAKE THE NOODLES

1 Sauté the eggplant over medium heat in the sesame oil and soy sauce until just tender.

2 Cook the soba noodles as directed on the package. Strain and rinse under cool water. Set aside.

TO MAKE THE VINAIGRETTE

While the soba is cooking, mix all the vinaigrette ingredients in a large bowl. Whisk well to combine.

TO SERVE

1 In the same large mixing bowl, gently toss the cooled soba noodles in the vinaigrette, then add the eggplant, red pepper, and arugula.

2 Coat all of the noodles well and serve with tongs, twisting the noodles when you serve them so they stay firm.

3 Top with crushed peanuts or Thai basil, if desired.

PER SERVING: 181 calories, 7 g fat (1 g saturated), 6 g protein, 1 g fiber, 3 g sugars, 427 mg sodium, 26 g carbohydrates

Made from buckwheat, soba noodles are the extra-sexy noodle! They contain selenium and zinc and help aid digestion. They're also a slow-release carb. Get smart and switch up to nutrient-dense noodle varieties.

"Vegetables are a
must on a diet. I suggest
carrot cake, zucchini bread,
and pumpkin pie."
Jim Davis

CHAPTER 9

Veggie Mains

Dearest Meat: It's not that I

don't love you anymore. It's just that for too long, you've been
the star of every dish. It's time to step aside and introduce a
new main act. These fresh, veggie main dishes keep me svelte
and satisfied 5 nights a week. (Don't you worry, Meat, we'll see
each other as a special treat—only on the weekends.)

roasted cauliflower and leek soup

THIS CREAMY SOUP IS ONE OF my favorite starters to any holiday meal. It has a luxurious, velvety texture that's not only delicious, it's straight-up sexy.

FWB: Cauliflower, garlic

Makes 4 servings

1 garlic head

2 tablespoons extra-virgin olive oil, divided

1 cauliflower head, cut into 1-inch pieces

2 large leeks, trimmed, halved, and sliced into half-moons

½ teaspoon sea salt + more to taste

3½ cups chicken stock, or veggie stock to veganize

1 cup unsweetened almond milk

Fresh sage, fresh thyme, or freshly grated whole nutmeg, to garnish (optional)

1 To roast the garlic, preheat the oven to 350°F. Cut the garlic in half horizontally, drizzle with 1 teaspoon olive oil, and tent with aluminum foil. Roast for 1 hour, and then set aside to cool. Remove the cloves from their skins.

2 Lightly oil a large baking sheet and spread out the cauliflower and leek pieces to cover the pan. Drizzle with the remaining olive oil and ½ teaspoon sea salt. Roast in a 350° oven for 1 hour, or until soft and golden.

3 In a food processor or blender, combine the roasted vegetables and peeled garlic cloves. Begin to pulse and puree. Slowly add the stock in small batches until you achieve a velvety consistency.

4 Add the almond milk to finish, blending well.

5 Place the soup in a medium saucepan over medium heat to warm it through. Stir in sea salt to taste.

6 Garnish with the sage, thyme, or nutmeg, if desired.

PER SERVING: 235 calories, 11 g fat (2 g saturated), 10 g protein, 4 g fiber, 8 g sugars, 561 mg sodium, 27 g carbohydrates

KEEP IT SEXY: No leeks available? Opt for 4 mild green onions or half a yellow onion and 1 green onion.

roasted garlic–lentil soup

LENTILS HAVE TO BE THE WORLD'S most fiber-filled legume. They'll keep you fuller longer, aid digestion, and give you a vibrant, gorgeous glow. So eat yourself healthy and beautiful with this fragrant soup.

FWB: Garlic, Swiss chard

Makes 6 servings

2 garlic heads

1 tablespoon extra-virgin olive oil

2 tablespoons canola oil

4 ounces pancetta (optional), cut into cubes

1 yellow onion, chopped

1 medium parsnip, peeled and chopped

2 carrots, peeled and chopped

2 fresh thyme sprigs

1 bay leaf

1½ cups brown, red, or green lentils

8 cups chicken stock, divided

½ large bunch Swiss chard, chopped

¼ teaspoon sea salt

1 Preheat the oven to 350°F. Cut the garlic in half horizontally, drizzle with 1 teaspoon olive oil, and tent with aluminum foil. Roast for 1 hour and set aside to cool. Remove the cloves from their skins.

2 Coat the bottom of a large Dutch oven or stockpot with the canola oil. Add the pancetta (if using) and sauté over medium heat until crispy, about 4 minutes. Remove from the pot using a slotted spoon, place on a paper towel, and reserve.

3 Add the onion to the pot and sauté until fragrant and translucent, about 6 minutes. Add the parsnip, carrots, thyme sprigs, and bay leaf and cook for 5 more minutes.

4 Add the lentils and 6 cups of the chicken stock. Bring to a boil, cover, and gently simmer for 25 to 30 minutes, or until the lentils are soft.

5 When the soup is ready, mix in the Swiss chard, sea salt, reserved roasted garlic, and pancetta (if using). Simmer on low heat until the chard is just wilted, about 10 minutes. Add the remaining 2 cups chicken stock after the Swiss chard wilts, to finish.

PER SERVING: 238 calories, 8 g fat (1 g saturated), 11 g protein, 11 g fiber, 2 g sugars, 1,047 mg sodium, 31 g carbohydrates

I am in love with adding parsnips to my soups. Parsnips always cook up perfectly in simmering stock; their mild, sweet, fragrant, earthy flavor comforts me to my core.

dreamy butternut squash mac 'n' cheese

WHO DOESN'T LOVE A BOWL of warm, creamy mac 'n' cheese? Now you can enjoy a satisfying and mouthwatering version with zero guilt. This may be the perfect recipe to cook yourself sexy and happy!

FWB: Butternut squash

Makes 6 servings

MAC 'N' CHEESE

2½ pounds butternut squash, peeled, halved, and seeded, then quartered and sliced into triangles

6 garlic cloves

1 thyme sprig

2 cups unsweetened almond milk

2 cups chicken stock, or vegetable stock to veganize

1 pound small elbow macaroni or mini shells

2 tablespoons grated Gruyère

HERBED BREADCRUMB TOPPING

¾ cup panko breadcrumbs

1 tablespoon finely chopped flat-leaf parsley

2 garlic cloves, minced

¼ teaspoon sea salt

TO MAKE THE MAC 'N' CHEESE

1 Preheat the oven to 375°F. In a large saucepan, add the butternut squash, garlic cloves, thyme sprig, unsweetened almond milk, and stock. Cook until the butternut squash is fork-tender. Remove the sprig of thyme.

2 Place the squash mixture in a food processor or blender and puree until velvety smooth.

3 Meanwhile, cook the macaroni in salted water until it is al dente (semifirm). Drain and rinse with cool water.

4 Spread out the macaroni in a lightly greased 13-inch × 9-inch pan. Pour the squash puree over the noodles.

TO MAKE THE BREADCRUMBS AND BAKE

1 Combine all the ingredients for the herbed breadcrumb topping.

2 Cover the mac 'n' cheese with foil, place in the oven, and bake for approximately 45 minutes. Remove from the oven and evenly spread the breadcrumb topping and Gruyère over the top. Transfer to the broiler and broil for 5 to 10 minutes, or until the cheese is brown and bubbly.

PER SERVING: 443 calories, 5 g fat (1 g saturated), 16 g protein, 6 g fiber, 10 g sugars, 280 mg sodium, 86 g carbohydrates

Want to veganize this dish? Opt for veggie stock, swap in almond cheese, and add fresh herbs like thyme, parsley, or even double the garlic.

grilled mushroom and leek flatbread pizza

IF YOU'RE PIZZA OBSESSED LIKE I AM, you'll devour this recipe. With a crisp crust and intensely robust mushrooms, onions, and leeks, it's pretty much perfection. I serve this paired with a Pinot Grigio and my Caramelized French Onion Soup (page 79) or cut into small bites as an app.

FWB: Mushrooms, onion

Makes 6 servings

- 2 tablespoons + 2 teaspoons extra-virgin olive oil, divided
- 1 small yellow onion, halved and thinly sliced
- 2 tablespoons balsamic vinegar
- 2 cups cremini mushrooms, thinly sliced, preferably on a mandoline
- 1 leek, halved, rinsed, and finely chopped
- 2½ teaspoons sea salt, divided
- All-purpose flour for rolling dough
- 1 pound store-bought pizza dough
- 2 tablespoons grated Parmesan cheese
- ¼ cup basil leaves

1. In a large skillet, heat 2 tablespoons of the olive oil over medium heat. Add the onion, reduce the heat to low, and cook, stirring occasionally.

2. Add the balsamic vinegar once the onion has picked up some color. Continue to cook the onion until fully caramelized, approximately 20 minutes. (If the onion slices start to stick to the pan, splash the pan with a bit of water and stir and scrape up any browned bits.)

3. Increase the heat to medium. Stir in the mushrooms and cook until they just begin to soften and lose their moisture, 2 to 4 minutes. Add the leek and 2 teaspoons of the salt and cook for an additional minute. Set aside.

4. Heat a charcoal or gas grill or a grill pan to medium-high heat. Sprinkle your work surface with flour and roll the dough into a ½-inch-thick circle. Brush the grill pan (or grill grates) with 1 teaspoon of the oil and gently lay the dough on the grates. Grill until the underside of the crust is golden, 1 to 2 minutes, and then use a spatula to flip the dough over.

5. Brush the remaining 1 teaspoon oil over the top of the dough and sprinkle with the remaining ½ teaspoon sea salt. Grill until the underside is golden, another 1 to 2 minutes. Transfer the grilled pizza round to a cutting board.

(continued)

6 Top the pizza base with the mushroom and leek mixture. Sprinkle with the Parmesan cheese and finish with a few leaves of basil before slicing and serving.

PER SERVING: 369 calories, 8 g fat (1 g saturated), 10 g protein, 3 g fiber, 5 g sugars, 829 mg sodium, 65 g carbohydrates

BENEFIT THAT BOD: Try cutting your oil and cheese amounts in half. Instead, boost the flavor by adding roasted garlic, sun-dried tomatoes, more caramelized onions, or fresh herbs.

candice's homemade marinara sauce

THIS SIMPLE, CLASSIC RECIPE WILL QUICKLY become your go-to sauce— tack it to your fridge, or save it front and center in your recipe folder. Just say no to the preservatives, added sugars, fillers, and corn syrup found in most jarred sauces. Savor this fresh, delicious, and simple homemade marinara!

FWB: Tomatoes, basil

Makes 4 servings

1 yellow onion, chopped

2 tablespoons extra-virgin olive oil

4 garlic cloves, minced

2 (28-ounce) cans organic diced tomatoes

¼ cup chopped fresh basil

2 sprigs fresh oregano or 2 tablespoons dried

¼ cup balsamic vinegar or red wine

¼ teaspoon sea salt, or to taste

1 In a large saucepan, sauté the onion in the olive oil for approximately 20 minutes over low heat. Add the garlic and sauté for another 10 minutes.

2 Add the tomatoes and herbs. Mix well and cook on low for approximately 2 hours.

3 When the sauce has thickened, finish it off with a touch of balsamic vinegar or red vino and allow it to simmer for about 5 more minutes.

4 Finish off with the sea salt. Enjoy over a delicious bowl of buttery pasta, lasagna noodles, or whole wheat penne. Simple, wasn't it? *Buon appetito!*

PER SERVING: 189 calories, 7 g fat (1 g saturated), 4 g protein, 4 g fiber, 16 g sugars, 971 mg sodium, 26 g carbohydrates

lemon-basil lasagna rolls

DID YOU KNOW THAT 1 SERVING of the average frozen lasagna contributes a whopping 30% of your daily saturated fat and cholesterol, plus 12 grams of fat? Yikes! Try these smart, sexy lasagna rolls instead—you'll save your waistline and your wallet!

FWB: Oregano, basil

Makes 6 servings

12–15 lasagna noodles

2½ cups Candice's Homemade Marinara Sauce (page 133), divided

1 (15-ounce) container part-skim ricotta cheese

Zest of 2 lemons

1 tablespoon chopped fresh oregano

1 cup julienned fresh basil

1 teaspoon sea salt

Additional lemon zest and fresh oregano or basil, for garnish

KEEP IT SEXY: For an even healthier twist, cut out half of the ricotta cheese mixture and swap in sautéed vegetables, such as mushrooms, asparagus, and Swiss chard. You'll still get the hit of comfort food with all the sauce. Just add a little grated Parmesan cheese on top.

1 Preheat the oven to 350°F.

2 Cook the lasagna noodles in a large pot of boiling water per package directions until just shy of al dente. Drain and immediately rinse under cold water to stop the cooking process.

3 Cover the bottom of a 13-inch × 9-inch baking dish with 1 cup of the marinara sauce.

4 In a medium bowl, blend the ricotta, lemon zest, oregano, basil, and sea salt.

5 On a clean work surface, spread out 4 noodles. Top with roughly 2 tablespoons of the ricotta mixture, spreading evenly over each noodle to create a thin layer for less mess.

6 Roll each noodle tightly across to make a compact spiral. Repeat with all remaining noodles.

7 Place the rolled noodles neatly in the baking dish and cover with the remaining 1½ cups sauce. Bake uncovered on the center rack for 30 minutes.

8 Garnish with additional lemon zest and fresh oregano or basil.

PER SERVING: 422 calories, 8 g fat (4 g saturated), 17 g protein, 3 g fiber, 6 g sugars, 510 mg sodium, 68 g carbohydrates

spinach and mushroom pierogies

BEING HALF JAPANESE AND HALF POLISH not only makes me a megahard worker, it motivates me to create insane dumplings! This pierogi recipe is inspired by my lovely Babcia and Jadzia, aka my Polish grandma and aunt: Thanks for all the years of amazing food, hospitality, and love. I learned from the best.

FWB: Mushrooms, spinach

Makes 24 pierogies

DOUGH

2 eggs

¼ cup light sour cream

1 cup water

1 teaspoon sea salt

3½ cups sifted all-purpose flour, divided

FILLING

1 tablespoon extra-virgin olive oil

½ large or 1 medium yellow onion, finely chopped

2 garlic cloves, finely minced

3 cups finely chopped cremini mushrooms

1 cup baby spinach leaves

2 tablespoons chopped fresh parsley

1 teaspoon sea salt, or to taste

1 tablespoon canola oil

TOPPINGS

¼ cup light sour cream

2 green onions, finely chopped on the bias

TO MAKE THE DOUGH

1 In a medium mixing bowl, whisk the eggs, sour cream, water, and sea salt. Gently rain in the 3¼ cups sifted flour, 1 cup at a time, until fully incorporated.

2 Turn out the dough onto a lightly floured work surface and knead gently until smooth. Place the dough in a lightly oiled bowl, cover it with a damp paper towel, and allow the dough to rest in the fridge for approximately 20 minutes.

TO MAKE THE FILLING

1 In a medium sauté pan over medium heat, add the olive oil and yellow onion and sauté until soft and fragrant, about 8 to 10 minutes. Add the garlic and cook for 2 more minutes.

2 Add the mushrooms, tossing well to coat, and cook for about 10 minutes. Fold in the spinach, cooking just to wilt. Add the parsley and season with the sea salt. Cool slightly before assembling.

TO ASSEMBLE

1 Remove the dough from the refrigerator and place it on a well-floured work surface. Set a small bowl of water next to your work area. Roll out the dough to approximately ¼ inch thick. Cut out dough rounds using a 3- to 4-inch round biscuit cutter (or use the rim of a drinking

glass). Place about 1 to 2 teaspoons of the filling in the center of each circle. Dip your fingers in the water and moisten the edge of half of the circle, then fold the other half over to make a half-moon shape. Press and seal the edges together using the back of a fork.

2 Transfer the dumplings to a rimmed baking sheet dusted with flour and repeat with the remaining dough and filling. Cover the baking sheet with plastic wrap and chill the pierogies for 30 minutes or up to 2 hours. (Or freeze them in a single layer on a baking sheet, and then transfer them to a resealable freezer bag for up to 6 months. The pierogies can be added to boiling water straight from the freezer.)

3 Set a large sauté pan over medium heat. Add the canola oil, then about 10 dumplings (taking care not to overcrowd the pan), and cook for 2 minutes on each side. Remove them with a spatula and place them on a paper towel–lined plate to remove any excess oil. Continue until the remaining pierogies are cooked. Serve topped with the light sour cream and green onions.

If you prefer lighter pierogies, steam or boil them as you would pot stickers or dumplings. You'll save calories and inches, one batch at a time!

PER SERVING: 91 calories, 2 g fat (0.5 g saturated), 3 g protein, 1 g fiber, 0 g sugars, 208 mg sodium, 15 g carbohydrates

homemade veggie burgers

WHO SAYS YOU HAVE TO PURCHASE processed or frozen veggie burgers? With chickpeas, whole rolled oats, and walnuts, which are loaded with protein and omega-3 fatty acids, these homemade winners will make you say ciao to premade burgers. They're delicious served over a bed of greens or dressed up in a pita pocket with arugula and apple slices.

FWB: Chickpeas, cumin

Makes 4 servings

1 (15-ounce) can chickpeas, drained

½ cup finely chopped shallots

1 cup rolled oats

½ cup walnut pieces

½ teaspoon ground cumin

1 teaspoon ground turmeric (optional)

2 tablespoons reduced-sodium soy sauce

2 tablespoons fresh oregano (optional)

1 tablespoon canola oil

1 In a food processor, combine the chickpeas, shallots, rolled oats, walnuts, cumin, turmeric (if using), soy sauce, and oregano (if using). Pulse for approximately 30 seconds, or until completely combined.

2 Shape the mixture into small, round patties and set aside.

3 In a large skillet, heat the canola oil over medium heat and cook the patties for 2 to 3 minutes on each side, or until they are golden brown. Serve in pita or enjoy over mixed greens.

PER SERVING: 284 calories, 15 g fat (1 g saturated), 10 g protein, 5 g fiber, 3 g sugars, 608 mg sodium, 29 g carbohydrates

BENEFIT THAT BOD: If you hate oregano or aren't a fan of cumin, go ahead and substitute your favorite herbs and spices instead. This burger has no limits, rules, or boundaries!

the think-pink salad

WHETHER OR NOT IT'S YOUR FAVORITE hue, there's a time for all girls to think pink. With 2 pounds of roasted beets, along with quinoa, arugula, and chèvre, you can't go wrong with this naturally pink recipe!

FWB: Beets, quinoa

Makes 4 servings

2 pounds beets, stems removed

4 tablespoons extra-virgin olive oil, divided

1½ cups arugula

2 cups cooked quinoa

3 tablespoons freshly squeezed lemon juice, divided

2 tablespoons chèvre (goat cheese)

¼ teaspoon sea salt

1 Preheat the oven to 425°F.

2 Use 1 tablespoon of the olive oil to coat the skin of the beets. Wrap each beet completely with aluminum foil. Roast until fork-tender, about 1 hour. Set aside to cool.

3 In a large bowl, combine the arugula and quinoa. Dress lightly with 2 tablespoons each of the olive oil and lemon juice. Toss to combine.

4 When the beets are cool, peel them, halve them, and cut them into half-moons. Add them to the salad and toss gently to incorporate. Top with the crumbled chèvre.

5 Drizzle the salad with the remaining olive oil and lemon juice. Finish with a sprinkle of sea salt.

PER SERVING: 355 calories, 18 g fat (3 g saturated), 9 g protein, 9 g fiber, 16 g sugars, 296 mg sodium, 43 g carbohydrates

Don't want a mess of hot-pink hands? Wear plastic gloves while peeling your beets. Keep it clean, keep it sexy.

warm fennel and arugula salad

ONE OF MY FAVORITE CHANGE-UPS ON the dinner table is a *warm* salad. Trust me! With the right ingredients and know-how, you'll impress your loved ones with this warm yet crisp and delightful mix.

FWB: Pomegranate, arugula

Makes 4 servings

POM VINAIGRETTE

¼ cup POM juice

2 tablespoons extra-virgin olive oil

¼ teaspoon sea salt

1 tablespoon balsamic vinegar

1 tablespoon Dijon mustard

SALAD

1 fennel bulb

1 tablespoon canola oil

1 teaspoon sea salt

1 cup peas, fresh or frozen

3 cups arugula

¼ cup shaved Asiago or Parmesan cheese

TO MAKE THE VINAIGRETTE

In a small bowl, combine all the ingredients for the vinaigrette.

TO MAKE THE SALAD

1 Preheat the oven to 400°F.

2 Thinly slice the fennel bulb, preferably on a mandoline. Toss the slices with the canola oil, place them on a baking sheet, and sprinkle them with sea salt.

3 Place the fennel in the oven to roast for 30 minutes.

4 In the meantime, thaw the peas (if frozen) and cook as directed on the package.

5 In a large mixing bowl, combine the arugula, peas, and half of the roasted fennel. Toss with half of the vinaigrette.

6 Transfer the salad to 4 plates. Top with the remaining fennel. Using a vegetable peeler, thinly slice ribbons of the cheese over each salad. Serve the remaining vinaigrette on the side.

PER SERVING: 171 calories, 13 g fat (3 g saturated), 4 g protein, 3 g fiber, 3 g sugars, 436 mg sodium, 11 g carbohydrates

KEEP IT SEXY: Don't have any POM juice on hand? Use cranberry or even apple juice.

roasted summer corn and avocado salad

WHENEVER IT'S COLD AND RAINY in New York City, all it takes is a quick batch of this corn salad to feel like I'm back in sunny California. There's nothing quite like roasted corn on the cob. Warm up with this perfect summer salad anytime of the year.

FWB: Avocado

Makes 6 servings

CREAMY DILL VINAIGRETTE

¼ cup + 1 tablespoon lemon juice

2 tablespoons extra-virgin olive oil

½ teaspoon sea salt

1 tablespoon 0% Greek yogurt

1 teaspoon fresh dill

½ teaspoon Mexican chili powder

½ teaspoon smoked paprika

SALAD

2 corn ears, charred on the grill or stove top

1 medium jicama

1 English hothouse cucumber, unpeeled

2 tablespoons chopped fresh dill, stems removed

1 ripe avocado, cut into small cubes

Dill sprigs, to garnish

TO MAKE THE VINAIGRETTE

In a small bowl, whisk together all the ingredients for the vinaigrette.

TO MAKE THE SALAD

1 Remove the charred corn kernels from the cobs by placing the cobs on a clean work surface and shaving off all sides, using a serrated knife. Place them in a large bowl.

2 Thinly slice the jicama and cucumber, preferably on a mandoline, and julienne them.

3 Into the bowl of corn kernels, add the jicama, cucumber, and dill. Toss gently with half of the vinaigrette until thoroughly combined. Finish by adding in the avocado cubes. Serve garnished with dill sprigs and with extra dressing on the side.

PER SERVING: 155 calories, 9 g fat (1 g saturated), 3 g protein, 8 g fiber, 5 g sugars, 170 mg sodium, 20 g carbohydrates

NOTE: If fresh corn isn't in season, canned corn is a fine substitute. Remember to drain well and cook in a grill pan over medium heat. When char marks appear, remove from the heat and follow the recipe.

"I don't like gourmet cooking or
'this' cooking or 'that' cooking.
I like good cooking."
James Beard

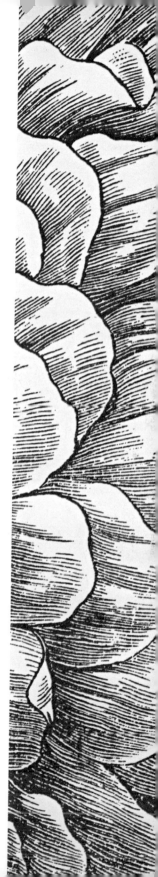

CHAPTER 10

Sexier Sides

Ah yes, the side dish. Similar to the fifth wheel or the middle child, the side dish doesn't get as much love as it should. Allow me to introduce these sexy stars. You'll find savory Rosemary Garlic Fries, decadent Roasted Miso- and Honey-Glazed Parsnips, and sweet Maple-Glazed Butternut Squash. You'll feel satisfied but never stuffed after this sideshow!

sautéed broccoli raab with chili flakes

BROCCOLINI (AKA BROCCOLI RAAB) IS LIKE the hip, younger sis of broccoli and asparagus. Slightly similar in texture to asparagus, yet crisp and mildly sweet, this veggie will leave you feeling like a Brooklynite.

FWB: Broccoli raab

Serves 4

2 tablespoons extra-virgin olive oil

½ red onion, finely chopped

2 garlic cloves, finely minced

1 pound broccoli raab (broccolini), chopped into 1½" pieces

1 teaspoon chili flakes, or to taste

½ teaspoon sea salt

2 teaspoons fresh lemon juice (optional)

1   Heat the olive oil in a medium sauté pan over medium heat, and add the red onion. Sauté just until fragrant, approximately 5 minutes. Add the garlic and cook for another 2 minutes.

2   Add the broccoli raab, and sauté over medium heat for approximately 2 minutes, and then add the chili flakes and cook for another 3 minutes.

3   Remove from the heat and add the sea salt and a squeeze of lemon juice to finish, if desired.

PER SERVING: 97 calories, 8 g fat (1 g saturated), 4 g protein, 3 g fiber, 1 g sugars, 235 mg sodium, 5 g carbohydrates

BENEFIT THAT BOD: Getting tired of the same ol' veggies? Discover new and exciting produce like broccoli raab, daikon radish, Serrano chile peppers, watercress, Mizuna. Go green and get sexy!

Don't have broccoli raab available at your local grocer? Go ahead and swap it out for sliced broccoli or asparagus. Cook the same and voilà! Instant success!

cinnamon-sugar baked sweet potatoes

IF YOU'VE RULED OUT POTATOES BECAUSE you think they are bad for you, think again! These babies are sweet, satisfying, and bursting with vitamin A and beta-carotene.

FWB: Sweet potatoes

Makes 6 servings

6 large sweet potatoes or yams
2 teaspoons ground cinnamon
¼ cup organic sugar
3 tablespoons butter
Sea salt to taste

1 Preheat the oven to 350°F. Place the sweet potatoes or yams on a large baking sheet, poke them with a fork, and bake for about 45 minutes, or until tender.

2 While the potatoes are baking away, make a batch of cinnamon sugar by combining—you guessed it—the cinnamon and sugar. Phew!

3 When the potatoes are baked, remove them from the oven and allow them to cool before handling. When slightly cool to the touch, cut an X in the middle of each potato and push the fluffy, steamy insides to the top.

4 Add a pat (about ¼ to ½ tablespoon) of real butter to each potato and allow it to melt. (Every now and then, you should indulge. Just go for a run or a nice long stroll after.)

5 Sprinkle with cinnamon sugar and sea salt. Enjoy! Perfect for a semisavory dessert or a side dish for the holidays.

PER SERVING: 197 calories, 6 g fat (4 g saturated), 2 g protein, 4 g fiber, 14 g sugars, 113 mg sodium, 35 g carbohydrates

It is a good idea to cut out processed carbs, like white breads, crackers, cookies, and sweets. But sweet potatoes, baked potatoes, and mashed potatoes are healthy carbs! Prepare them with fresh, natural ingredients and enjoy.

maple-glazed butternut squash

THERE'S SOMETHING ABOUT THIS NUTTY, SWEET, decadent butternut squash that I can't get enough of. Try it paired with my Whole Roasted Go-To Chicken (page 181) or as a side dish at your next DIY dinner night or holiday dinner!

FWB: Butternut squash

Makes 4 servings

1 (2-pound) butternut squash, peeled, cut lengthwise, seeded, and sliced into ½-inch half-moons

2 tablespoons extra-virgin olive oil

2 tablespoons maple syrup

2 tablespoons finely chopped fresh sage

1 tablespoon finely chopped rosemary

1 tablespoon sea salt

1 Preheat the oven to 375°F. Line a baking sheet with aluminum foil.

2 In a large mixing bowl, toss together the butternut squash, olive oil, maple syrup, herbs, and sea salt.

3 Spread the mixture evenly across the baking sheet and roast for 45 minutes, or until the squash is fork-tender and the edges are crispy.

PER SERVING: 173 calories, 7 g fat (1 g saturated), 2 g protein, 4 g fiber, 10 g sugars, 407 mg sodium, 29 g carbohydrates

KEEP IT SEXY: Roasting butternut squash is as simple as peel, chop, toss, and roast. Packed with vitamins A and C and fiber, this is one hot dish.

smashed fingerling potatoes

MASHED POTATOES MAY SOUND BORING, BUT these little babies are "smashed," giving them a little extra oomph—and they're simple to make. Plus, they're a great stress reliever! Mash and smash these away to ease your soul and your stomach.

FWB: Potatoes

Makes 4 to 6 servings

2 pounds fingerling, baby russet, or blue potatoes
2 tablespoons fresh thyme
2 tablespoons extra-virgin olive oil
1 teaspoon sea salt

1 Preheat the oven to 350°F. Line a baking sheet with aluminum foil.

2 Wash and completely dry all of the potatoes. Using a fork, poke holes in all of the potatoes, and preroast them whole for 30 minutes, until just tender. Remove the potatoes from the oven and carefully smash them using a fork or the back of a measuring cup to form a flat, rustic shape.

3 Sprinkle the potatoes with olive oil, salt, and thyme leaves. Toss well to coat evenly. Return them to the oven for approximately 20 to 25 minutes. Roast until the potatoes become crisp and golden brown.

PER SERVING: 251 calories, 7 g fat (1 g saturated), 5 g protein, 3 g fiber, 0 g sugars, 333 mg sodium, 40 g carbohydrates

KEEP IT SEXY: Don't see any fingerlings? Check out the varieties of potatoes at your local farmers market! I love baby reds and blues. Mash and smash them with extra garlic and rosemary for a flavorful new take on this side dish.

rosemary-garlic fries with agave-shallot ketchup

OF COURSE YOU CAN HAVE FRENCH FRIES—just not at every meal! These garlicky fries are a special treat and the perfect pairing with the Better Burger (page 185). You'll love this divine roasted combo.

FWB: Potatoes, tomatoes

Makes 4 to 6 servings

KETCHUP

1 tablespoon extra-virgin olive oil

2 medium shallots or ½ yellow onion, finely minced

1 (28-ounce) can diced tomatoes

3 tablespoons agave nectar

⅓ cup apple cider vinegar

½ teaspoon sea salt

FRIES

3 pounds unpeeled russet potatoes, scrubbed

2 tablespoons butter

3 garlic cloves, finely minced

1 tablespoon finely chopped fresh rosemary

Sea salt, to taste

TO MAKE THE KETCHUP

1 In a large pot over medium heat, add the olive oil and sweat the shallots until soft and fragrant, about 8 minutes.

2 Add the diced tomatoes, agave, apple cider vinegar, and ½ teaspoon sea salt. Simmer uncovered over medium-low heat for approximately 1½ hours, or until thickened.

3 Remove from the heat. Place in a food processor or blender and blend until smooth.

TO MAKE THE FRIES

1 Preheat the oven to 375°F and line a baking sheet with aluminum foil.

2 Cut the potatoes into ½-inch-thick matchsticks.

3 In a small saucepan, melt the butter over low heat and add the garlic. Sauté until fragrant, approximately 2 minutes. Add the rosemary and let it infuse for 1 minute.

4 In a large bowl, toss the potatoes with the warm rosemary butter and garlic mixture. Evenly spread the coated potatoes on the baking sheet. Sprinkle with sea salt. Bake for approximately 50 minutes, or until the potatoes are golden brown.

5 Crank up the oven to 500°F. Bake the fries for an additional 5 minutes, or until crispy. Serve up with Agave-Shallot Ketchup.

PER SERVING: 480 calories, 9 g fat (4 g saturated), 10 g protein, 6 g fiber, 22 g sugars, 698 mg sodium, 93 g carbohydrates

roasted miso- and honey-glazed parsnips

DEAREST PARSNIP, I KNOW YOU ARE often overlooked, but I've seen those lovely roots, and I know you are oh so sweet! Related to the carrot, you're perfect when lightly simmered, roasted, braised, or even grilled. With the sweet addition of miso and honey, you can't go wrong with this subtle side.

FWB: Parsnips

Makes 4 servings

2 tablespoons miso paste (red or white)

2 tablespoons honey

2 tablespoons rice wine vinegar

2 tablespoons roasted sesame oil

1½ pounds parsnips

1 Preheat the oven to 375°F. In a mixing bowl, combine the first 4 ingredients to make the marinade, whisking well to incorporate.

2 Peel and slice the parsnips on the bias into ½-inch pieces.

3 Toss the parsnips in the marinade until they are well coated.

4 Allow the parsnips to marinate for about 20 minutes.

5 Place the parsnips on a large, foil-lined baking sheet and roast for approximately 45 minutes, or until they are tender but still crisp on the outside.

6 Serve with a miso-glazed salmon or miso-glazed tofu.

PER SERVING: 235 calories, 7 g fat (1 g saturated), 2 g protein, 10 g fiber, 18 g sugars, 333 mg sodium, 42 g carbohydrates

KEEP IT SEXY: Trying a new vegetable is like dating a different type of man. It's a little intimidating at first, but you might discover a whole new love affair! In addition to cooking with parsnips, change up your everyday meals and try some new, exotic veggies like kale, leeks, mizuna, or artichokes.

curried cauliflower

IF YOU HAVEN'T PLAYED WITH CURRY yet, well then, honey, get with it! Curry is packed with anti-inflammatory, anticancer, antibacterial, and possibly even antidepressant properties. It's time to dive into the curry powder and reap the benefits of this ultravibrant, brightly colored spice mixture.

FWB: Cauliflower

Makes 4 servings

1 tablespoon curry powder

2 tablespoons canola oil

1 tablespoon lemon juice

1 teaspoon agave nectar

½ teaspoon sea salt

1 cauliflower head, chopped into 1-inch pieces

½ yellow onion, chopped

¼ cup dried cranberries

1 Preheat the oven to 375°F.

2 In a medium mixing bowl, add the curry powder, canola oil, lemon juice, agave, and sea salt. Whisk well to combine.

3 Add the cauliflower and onion to the marinade and toss to coat evenly.

4 Place the seasoned cauliflower and onion on a large baking sheet lined with foil. Roast for about 45 minutes or until golden brown.

5 After roasting, mix in the dried cranberries and enjoy this side perfectly paired with creamy Lemon-Caper Salmon with Greek Yogurt (page 170) or Whole Roasted Go-To Chicken (page 181).

PER SERVING: 138 calories, 7 g fat (1 g saturated), 3 g protein, 4 g fiber, 10 g sugars, 242 mg sodium, 17 g carbohydrates

The turmeric in curry powder gives it that bright yellow color and also helps relieve bloating, jaundice, bruising, menstrual cramps, toothaches, and chest pain. Fix what ails you naturally, sister, by reaching for some curry in a hurry!

dijon-braised brussels sprouts

IF YOU HATED BRUSSELS SPROUTS AS a kid, it's time to grow up and redis-cover this amazing food. This vegetable is packed with vitamins B_1, B_6, C, and K, as well as folate, fiber, and potassium. You'll go crazy over these Dijon-braised Brussels sprouts and wonder why you waited so long to devour them!

FWB: Brussels sprouts, almonds, apricots

Makes 4 servings

VINAIGRETTE
2 tablespoons Dijon mustard
2 tablespoons extra-virgin olive oil
2 tablespoons apple cider vinegar
1 tablespoon honey
½ teaspoon sea salt

BRUSSELS SPROUTS
1 pound Brussels sprouts, julienned
½ cup slivered almonds
½ cup julienned dried apricots

TO MAKE THE VINAIGRETTE

In a small bowl, whisk together all the ingredients for the vinaigrette.

TO MAKE THE BRUSSELS SPROUTS

1 Preheat the oven to 350°F and line a baking sheet with aluminum foil.

2 In a large bowl, combine the Brussels sprouts, almonds, and apricots.

3 Pour the vinaigrette over the Brussels sprouts and toss well to combine.

4 Spread the mixture evenly on the baking sheet. Roast for approximately 55 minutes, or until the leaves of the sprouts are tender and golden brown.

PER SERVING: 252 calories, 14 g fat (2 g saturated), 7 g protein, 7 g fiber, 16 g sugars, 407 mg sodium, 30 g carbohydrates

KEEP IT FABULOUS: If you don't have dried apricots on hand, opt for dried cranberries or apple slices to add more tartness.

roasted tomatoes with barley

NOT ONLY DOES THIS RECIPE LOOK like it belongs on the cover of *Bon Appétit*, it tastes like it, too. I pride myself on developing recipes that make you feel sexy from the inside out! If you're not already familiar with barley, it will become your favorite new grain, keeping you slim, sexy, and satisfied.

FWB: Tomatoes, barley

Makes 4 servings

ROASTED TOMATOES

2 cups cherry tomatoes on the vine

2 tablespoons extra-virgin olive oil

2 tablespoons balsamic vinegar

1½ cups barley

3½–3¾ cups water

2 cups mizuna greens or arugula

1 cup thinly shaved fennel

2 tablespoons chèvre (goat cheese)

DIJON VINAIGRETTE

2 tablespoons extra-virgin olive oil

1 tablespoon Dijon mustard

2 tablespoons red wine vinegar

¼ teaspoon sea salt

TO MAKE THE ROASTED TOMATOES

1 Preheat the oven to 350°F. Place the tomatoes on the vine in a 13-inch × 9-inch roasting pan. Coat with the olive oil and balsamic vinegar and roast for 45 minutes.

2 While the tomatoes are in the oven, begin to cook the barley. Put the water in a medium saucepan over medium heat and cook the barley until it is fully cooked and slightly firm to the tooth.*

TO MAKE THE DIJON VINAIGRETTE

In a small bowl, whisk together all the ingredients for the vinaigrette.

TO SERVE

1 In a large salad bowl, combine the cooked barley, greens, and fennel. Toss gently with half of the vinaigrette. Place in a large serving bowl.

2 Serve the salad topped with the roasted tomatoes on the vine and crumbled chèvre. Serve with additional vinaigrette as needed.

PER SERVING: 440 calories, 16 g fat (3 g saturated), 10 g protein, 13 g fiber, 4 g sugars, 256 mg sodium, 65 g carbohydrates

To reduce cooking time by half, presoak your barley overnight. Unsoaked barley takes approximately 50 to 60 minutes of total cook time.

"A bottle of wine contains more philosophy than all the books in the world."

Louis Pasteur

CHAPTER 11

Skinny-Dip in the Sea

With more natural omega-3

fatty acids than any supplement, and more health bennies like lean protein, vitamin D, vitamin B$_{12}$, vitamin D, and magnesium than any slab of beef, many types of seafood offer a sustainable, effortless way to stay gorgeous from the inside out. Fish oil has also been linked to healthy skin, hair, and nails. Now that's a real beauty regimen if I've ever heard of one. Eat yourself gorgeous with delicious fish!

home-smoked orange trout*

A STOVETOP SMOKER IS THE NEXT best thing to a true wood-fired smoker, but in the sweet comfort of your own home. Enjoy this light fish over a bed of fresh greens or an antipasto, with a perfect pairing of Pinot Grigio.

FWB: Garlic, trout

Makes 4 servings

6 cups water

½ cup sea salt

⅓ cup brown sugar

2 shallots, thinly sliced, preferably on a mandoline

2 garlic cloves, crushed

2 tablespoons orange zest

2 thyme sprigs

2 whole (1–2-pound) trout, cleaned

2 teaspoons apple wood or cedar shavings

1 In a large resealable plastic container, combine the water, sea salt, brown sugar, shallots, garlic, orange zest, and thyme sprigs, stirring until the salt and sugar dissolve to create the brine.

2 Add the trout to the container, using a plate or weight to keep the trout submerged. Place the container in the refrigerator for 6 hours, or overnight.

3 Remove the trout from the brine and discard the liquid. Rinse and pat the trout dry with paper towels. Set aside.

4 Place the wood chips at the bottom of the stovetop smoker. Place the rack on top of the chips and the trout on the rack. Safely place the smoker over low heat directly on the stovetop for approximately 30 minutes, or until the fish is opaque and firm to the touch.

PER SERVING: 193 calories, 8 g fat (1.5 g saturated), 26 g protein, 0 g fiber, 1 g sugars, 1,012 mg sodium, 1 g carbohydrates

* *Recipe requires a stovetop smoker*

Don't limit yourself to just smoking fish. Check out the amazing recipe for Smoked Tofu and Edamame Bites on page 62.

crab, avocado, and fennel salad

A SIMPLE, DELICATE, AND HIGHLY ELEGANT salad for any occasion—the divine trio of fresh crab, rich and creamy avocado, and a fragrant touch of fennel will impress even the most discerning guest.

FWB: Avocado, fennel

Makes 4 servings

SALAD

1 fennel bulb

½ Fuji apple

2 cups arugula

1 semifirm avocado, cubed

⅓–½ cup high-quality fresh lump crabmeat (fresh is best, but if canned is your only option, go for it)

DRESSING

2 tablespoons lemon juice

2 tablespoons extra-virgin olive oil

1 teaspoon agave nectar

1 teaspoon dried oregano (optional)

¼ teaspoon sea salt

TO MAKE THE SALAD

1 Thinly slice the fennel bulb and Fuji apple, preferably on a mandoline.

2 In a large bowl, combine the arugula, shaved fennel, avocado, and apple slices.

3 Gently add the lump crabmeat and toss to incorporate.

TO MAKE THE DRESSING

1 Combine all the ingredients for the dressing. Whisk well to combine.

2 Pour just enough dressing over the salad to coat well. Gently toss and serve immediately.

PER SERVING: 173 calories, 13 g fat (2 g saturated), 5 g protein, 5 g fiber, 4 g sugars, 237 mg sodium, 13 g carbohydrates

Crab is a lean, lovely way to get high-quality protein and vitamins A, B_{12}, and C. It's also at low risk for mercury as well as low in calories, yet high in flavor.

pan-seared scallops in a creamy balsamic sauce

FULL OF VITAMIN B$_{12}$, ZINC, SELENIUM, and lean protein, scallops may be nature's perfect mollusk. No heavy cream here, just a simple swap for evaporated milk that will keep you (and your skinny jeans) happy.

FWB: Arugula, hazelnuts

Makes 6 servings

3 tablespoons butter, divided

2 shallots, thinly sliced, preferably on a mandoline

2 garlic cloves, smashed

¼ cup reduced-sodium soy sauce

⅓ cup balsamic vinegar

1 can (12 ounces) low-fat evaporated milk

1 (16-ounce) package linguine

1 pound scallops, cleaned, beards removed

Sea salt to taste

2 cups arugula

¼ cup crushed hazelnuts (optional)

1 In a medium saucepan over medium heat, add 1 tablespoon of the butter and sweat the shallots for approximately 5 minutes. Add the garlic and continue to cook until brown, approximately 2 to 3 minutes.

2 Add the soy sauce and balsamic vinegar to the pan and simmer over medium heat for a few minutes. Turn off the heat. Add 1 tablespoon of butter and stir until fully emulsified. Using a fine sieve, strain the sauce, discarding the shallots and garlic. Set aside to cool.

3 In a small saucepan over medium heat, add the evaporated milk and reduce it by half. Remove from the heat. Cool slightly. While the evaporated milk is reducing, cook the linguine as directed on the package. Strain, shock with cold water, and set aside.

4 In a medium sauté pan or cast-iron skillet over medium-high heat, add the remaining tablespoon of butter and the scallops. Cook them in the hot pan for approximately 2 to 3 minutes on each side.

5 To finish the sauce, combine the reduced evaporated milk with the balsamic/soy sauce mixture. Whisk to combine, and season with sea salt.

6 Lightly toss the linguine in the balsamic sauce, and toss in the arugula. Top with the crushed hazelnuts, and finally, the pan-seared scallops.

PER SERVING: 485 calories, 8 g fat (5 g saturated), 28 g protein, 2 g fiber, 12 g sugars, 839 mg sodium, 70 g carbohydrates

sweet honey chèvre and sardine flatbread pizza

SARDINES MIGHT BE ONE OF THE loves of my life. They're quite stunning on top of this flatbread pizza, all dressed up with honey chèvre, capers, and arugula—my kind of flashy fish!

FWB: Sardines, arugula

Makes 6 servings

PIZZA CRUST

3 tablespoons extra-virgin olive oil, divided

1 tablespoon all-purpose flour

1 pound ready-to-bake pizza dough

1 tablespoon sea salt

TOPPINGS

¼ cup + 2 tablespoons chèvre (goat cheese), divided

1 tablespoon honey

1 (4-ounce) can sardines in olive oil, drained

1½ cups arugula

¼ cup capers, drained

Pinch of sea salt

TO MAKE THE PIZZA CRUST

1 Preheat the oven to 375°F. Lightly grease a large baking sheet with 1 tablespoon of the olive oil.

2 Lightly flour a work surface. Using a rolling pin, shape the pizza dough into a rectangle large enough to reach all sides of the baking sheet. Lightly drizzle 1 tablespoon of olive oil over the pizza dough and sprinkle it with the sea salt.

3 Prebake the pizza dough for 15 minutes, until the bottom of the crust is firm and golden brown. Remove from the oven and allow to cool for 10 minutes.

TO MAKE THE TOPPINGS

1 Meanwhile, prepare the pizza toppings. In a small mixing bowl, blend ¼ cup of the chèvre with the honey until a smooth paste forms.

2 Once the crust is cool, spread the honey chèvre mix evenly over it. Arrange the sardines, arugula, and capers on top. Add small pats of the remaining 2 tablespoons chèvre.

(continued)

TO FINISH

1 Place the pizza back in the oven for 10 minutes and bake until the cheese is soft and the arugula has slightly wilted.

2 Garnish by drizzling the remaining 1 tablespoon olive oil and sprinkling a pinch of sea salt over the finished pizza. Slice into small wedges and serve directly off a cutting board.

PER SERVING: 315 calories, 15 g fat (3.5 g saturated), 12 g protein, 1 g fiber, 5 g sugars, 1,343 mg sodium, 37 g carbohydrates

KEEP IT FABULOUS: Don't love sardines as much as I do? Swap them out for marinated tofu cubes or grilled chicken, or add more fresh veggies like delicious roasted red bell peppers or sautéed mushrooms.

halibut en papillote

HERE'S THE SIMPLEST FISH RECIPE THAT will impress even the pickiest of eaters. Enjoy this dish paired with a sparkling white wine spritzer, my Orange and Avocado Citrus Salad on page 101, and my Sweet Peach Cobbler on page 211.

FWB: Fennel, Lemon

Makes 4 servings

2 cups shaved fennel, preferably sliced on a mandoline

2 tablespoons fennel fronds

2 teaspoons extra-virgin olive oil

1¼ teaspoons sea salt, divided

1 lemon, thinly sliced into rounds, preferably on a mandoline

4 fresh thyme sprigs

4 (4-ounce) halibut fillets

1 egg, lightly beaten, for egg wash

1 Preheat the oven to 450°F. Fold four 10-inch pieces of parchment paper in half. Cut each parchment into half a heart, keeping the folded side intact, so that when it is unfolded it forms a full heart.

2 In a medium bowl, combine the shaved fennel, fennel fronds, olive oil, and 1 teaspoon of the sea salt.

3 On one side of the heart-shaped parchment, place 3 lemon slices. Top the lemon slices with 1 sprig of thyme, followed by 1 halibut fillet, and season with the remaining sea salt.

4 Top each fillet with one-quarter of the fennel mixture.

5 Brush one edge of the parchment with the egg wash. Fold the empty half of the parchment over the fish. Starting at the top of the heart, begin making folds along the edge, brushing the paper with egg wash each time it is folded to create a packet with the fish enclosed. Each fold should overlap the previous one.

6 Place the halibut packets on a baking sheet and bake for 8 minutes.

7 Remove from the oven. Using a sharp scissors, cut an opening in the top of each packet, being extremely careful not to burn yourself on the steam. Fold the cut edges back to expose the fish. Serve and enjoy!

PER SERVING: 165 calories, 5 g fat (1 g saturated), 24 g protein, 2 g fiber, 1 g sugars, 476 mg sodium, 5 g carbohydrates

lemon-caper salmon with greek yogurt

AN EASY-TO-PREPARE DISH WITH SEVEN INGREDIENTS that cooks in 20 minutes or less? This recipe screams success! Baste and bake this salmon and serve it with my Kale and Fennel Caesar (page 99), and you'll still have time to shower, throw on that hot new dress, and pour the wine!

FWB: Salmon, yogurt

Makes 4 servings

1 tablespoon lemon juice
2 tablespoons capers
⅓ cup 0% Greek yogurt
1 tablespoon Worcestershire sauce
1 tablespoon Dijon mustard
4 (5-ounce) boneless salmon fillets
1 large shallot, finely minced

1 Preheat the oven to 350°F. Line a baking sheet with aluminum foil and lightly coat it with cooking spray.

2 In a small bowl, whisk together the lemon juice, capers, Greek yogurt, Worcestershire, and Dijon.

3 Place the salmon fillets skin side down on the baking sheet.

4 Using a pastry brush, generously baste each piece of salmon with the yogurt mixture.

5 After basting, toss the shallot pieces in the remaining Greek yogurt mixture until they are well coated and place some on top of each salmon fillet.

6 Place the baking sheet on the middle rack and bake for 20 minutes, or until the salmon is opaque at the edges and still pink at the very center.

PER SERVING: 327 calories, 19 g fat (4 g saturated), 31 g protein, 0 g fiber, 2 g sugars, 350 mg sodium, 6 g carbohydrates

BENEFIT THAT BOD: Bursting with vitamins B_3, B_{12}, and D, omega-3 fatty acids, and protein, salmon is not only easy to prepare, it'll make you feel like Superwoman from the inside out.

s'mega sardine sandwich

SWAP TUNA FISH SANDWICHES for a more sustainable, eco-friendly fish. Pacific sardines are packed with omegas that keep your brain sharp. Paired with creamy California avocado, crisp red onion, and lightly toasted sourdough, this sandwich is a no-brainer for smarties like us!

FWB: Sardines, arugula, avocado

Makes 6 small bites

DRESSING

1½ teaspoons balsamic vinegar

1½ teaspoons Dijon mustard

1 egg yolk

½ teaspoon sea salt

¼ teaspoon freshly ground black pepper

1½ teaspoons olive oil from the sardine can

1 cup arugula

SANDWICHES

1 tablespoon mayonnaise

4 slices sourdough bread, cut into 12 equal pieces

1 can (3.75–4 ounces) sardines

1 avocado, sliced

1 red onion, thinly sliced, preferably on a mandoline

TO MAKE THE DRESSING

In a small bowl, place all the ingredients for the dressing except the arugula. Whisk gently to combine. Lightly toss the arugula with the dressing. Use just enough dressing to coat the arugula lightly. Reserve.

TO MAKE THE SANDWICHES

1 Spread a thin layer of mayonnaise on half of the bread pieces. In a medium sauté pan, toast them mayo side down, along with the other 6 bread pieces.

2 Evenly divide the dressed arugula among the 6 bread pieces with mayo. Top with the sardines, avocado, and red onion and finish with your last 6 pieces of toasted bread. Absolutely delish!

PER SERVING: 239 calories, 10 g fat (2 g saturated), 10 g protein, 3 g fiber, 2 g sugars, 503 mg sodium, 28 g carbohydrates

Sardines have been linked to improved brain development and memory and can help protect your brain and nervous system—along with your hot bod! Eat better, feel better, look better.

clams in white wine sauce over buttered linguine

THIS SLIGHTLY SPICY TAKE ON CLASSIC linguine and clams is hearty but won't weigh you down. Once you see how simple it is to sauté, boil, and strain, you'll come back to this recipe as a household classic.

FWB: Clams, garlic

Makes 4 servings

2 dozen hard-shelled small clams or cockles

4 tablespoons butter

8 garlic cloves, thinly sliced

2 thyme sprigs

1 cup dry white wine (I love my Chardonnay or Pinot Grigio)

½ cup finely chopped Italian parsley + additional to garnish (optional)

1 teaspoon julienned fresh basil leaves

¼ teaspoon sea salt, or to taste

½ pound linguine (whole wheat is always a healthy option)

½ cup arugula

Chili flakes (optional)

Tabasco sauce (optional)

KEEP IT FABULOUS: Wait until just before serving the meal to toss in your fresh herbs, so they stay vibrant and green.

1 Clean and scrub the clams, discarding any open ones. In a large stockpot, heat the butter over low heat. Add the garlic and thyme sprigs and sauté just until fragrant.

2 Turn up the heat to medium-high and add the clams. Cover the pot and steam the clams until they open, about 5 to 8 minutes. Occasionally shake the pan to help them cook. Discard the stubborn (aka unopened) ones.

3 Turn down the heat to medium-low and remove the lid. Pour the wine over the clams and cook for 1 minute, until the flavors combine. Using a slotted spoon, remove the clams to a side dish and cover them to keep warm.

4 Cook the liquid until the wine reduces by one-third. Remove from the heat and stir in the parsley and basil. Add the sea salt.

5 Meanwhile, cook the linguine as directed on the box in a large stockpot or pasta pot of boiling salted water. When the pasta is al dente, strain it and rinse it with cold water. Toss the pasta gently in the sauce.

6 Using tongs, divide the pasta between 2 individual dinner plates. Arrange the clams around each plate. Top with arugula to finish. Serve with a little additional fresh parsley, chili flakes, or even Tabasco, if desired.

PER SERVING: 409 calories, 13 g fat (7.5 g saturated), 15 g protein, 2 g fiber, 3 g sugars, 219 mg sodium, 47 g carbohydrates

orange miso-glazed salmon over brown rice

THE SIMPLE INGREDIENTS MAKE THIS FANCY-LOOKING salmon recipe super-easy to prepare and enjoy. You'll find a new love for this popular fish with this Asian-inspired dish.

FWB: Salmon, brown rice

Makes 4 servings

2 tablespoons orange juice

2 tablespoons red or white miso paste

1 tablespoon rice wine vinegar

1 tablespoon agave nectar

2 teaspoons roasted sesame oil

4 (6-ounce, 1-inch-thick) salmon fillets, skin on

2 cups brown rice, uncooked

1 tablespoon toasted sesame seeds (optional)

2 green onions, trimmed and thinly sliced on the bias

1 Preheat the oven to 350°F. Whisk the orange juice and miso paste with the rice wine vinegar, agave, and roasted sesame oil to make a smooth paste.

2 Coat a 13-inch × 9-inch baking dish with cooking spray. Place the salmon fillets skin side down in the pan and brush them with about half of the marinade. Set aside for 10 minutes (or refrigerate for up to 1 hour) to marinate.

3 Brush the salmon with the rest of the marinade and bake until the salmon is opaque at the edges and still pink at the very center, approximately 20 minutes.

4 While the salmon is cooking, prepare the brown rice as directed on the package.

5 Remove the fish from the oven and cool for 5 minutes before sprinkling with the sesame seeds, if using, and the green onions. Serve alongside the brown rice, paired with steamed bok choy or the Roasted Miso- and Honey-Glazed Parsnips on page 154.

PER SERVING: 667 calories, 28 g fat (6 g saturated), 41 g protein, 3 g fiber, 6 g sugars, 477 mg sodium, 60 g carbohydrates

chili-lime shrimp tacos

GROWING UP IN SUNNY, GORGEOUS SAN DIEGO, I ate my share of great Mexican food. Try these tacos and you'll swear off packaged, take-out Mexican meals forever!

FWB: Shrimp, cabbage

Makes 4 servings

CHILI-LIME MARINADE

1 tablespoon lime juice

2 tablespoons reduced-sodium soy sauce

1 teaspoon chili powder

¼ teaspoon cumin

APPLE-CABBAGE SLAW

½ cup finely shredded red cabbage

½ cup finely shredded green cabbage

½ Fuji apple, finely chopped (into matchsticks)

Soy-Lime Vinaigrette (page 71)

TACOS

1 pound 21/25 shrimp, raw, peeled, deveined, drained

1 tablespoon extra-virgin olive oil

20 small corn tortillas

Juice of 1 lime (optional)

TO MAKE THE MARINADE

In a medium mixing bowl, combine the lime juice, soy sauce, chili powder, and cumin, and whisk well.

TO MAKE THE SLAW

Combine the chopped cabbage and apple in a bowl, and toss with 1 tablespoon of the Soy-Lime Vinaigrette.

TO MAKE THE TACOS

1 Add the shrimp to the chili-lime marinade, and toss well to coat.

2 Cover and marinate in the fridge for 20 to 30 minutes.

3 Heat the oil in a medium sauté pan over medium heat. When the pan is hot, add the shrimp and cook for approximately 5 minutes, or until firm and opaque. Place the shrimp in warmed tortillas. Top with cabbage slaw and fresh lime juice, if desired!

PER SERVING: 462 calories, 10 g fat (1 g saturated), 28 g protein, 8 g fiber, 4 g sugars, 484 mg sodium, 68 g carbohydrates

BENEFIT THAT BOD: Tacos don't have to be loaded with calories and fat. The use of fresh flavors like lime, chili, and an apple-cabbage slaw are a must-try makeover for regular messy, greasy tacos.

"A man's health can be judged
by which he takes two at a
time—pills or stairs."
Joan Welsh

CHAPTER 12

Date-Night Dinners for Two

I've served up plenty of date nights and dinner parties, and I've developed the following recipes that are guaranteed to have him falling head over heels. Try these decadent, sinful—yet guilt free!—meals for the two of you (or treat your friends to a fabulous meal). Revel in the passion of cooking a delicious dinner for someone else, and who knows? By the end of the night, you might be the one who's getting romanced!

pan-seared duck breast with fennel and kale salad

DUCK IS ONE OF THOSE THINGS most men will never attempt to cook on a date. So take charge and wow him with this simple pan sear that cooks itself to perfection! You'll be surprised at how simple and easy it is to execute, and how irresistible it tastes.

FWB: Kale, fennel

Makes 2 servings

SALAD
½ large bunch curly kale

1 fennel bulb

2 tablespoons fennel fronds, picked but not chopped

1 Fuji apple, thinly sliced, preferably on a mandoline

POM VINAIGRETTE
3 tablespoons POM juice

3 tablespoons extra-virgin olive oil

2 tablespoons balsamic vinegar

2 tablespoons Dijon mustard

Sea salt to taste

POM GLAZE
½ cup POM juice

1 teaspoon honey

DUCK
1 duck breast, skin on, lightly scored (see opposite page)

Sea salt to taste

Black pepper to taste

TO MAKE THE SALAD

1 Trim the stalks off the kale. Roll the leaves into a cigar shape and thinly slice them.

2 Trim the end and leafy tops off the fennel bulb, reserving the fronds. Thinly slice the bulb, preferably on a mandoline, and place it in a large bowl with the kale, sliced apples, and picked fennel fronds.

TO MAKE THE VINAIGRETTE

Combine all the ingredients for the vinaigrette in a small bowl. Pour the vinaigrette over the vegetables and toss to combine. This salad will hold well for 1 to 2 hours.

TO MAKE THE GLAZE

Heat the POM juice and honey in a small saucepan over medium-high heat. Reduce the liquid until it is thick and syrupy enough to coat the back of a spoon, being careful not to scorch the bottom of the pan.

TO MAKE THE DUCK

1 Preheat the oven to 350°F. Heat an oven-safe medium sauté pan over medium-low heat. Season the duck with salt and pepper. Place the duck breast skin side down in the pan. Cook for 5 to 8 minutes, rendering the fat, until crispy. Flip the breast over and continue cooking for about 2 more minutes. Finish off in the oven for about 8 minutes, or as needed.

2 Transfer the cooked duck to a cutting board. Let it rest
for 5 to 10 minutes. Slice on a bias into ½-inch pieces.
Divide the salad between 2 serving plates. Top with
slices of duck and drizzle with POM glaze. Garnish with
the reserved fennel fronds.

PER SERVING: 609 calories, 32 g fat (5 g saturated), 24 g protein,
11 g fiber, 26 g sugars, 587 mg sodium, 65 g carbohydrates

SCORING A DUCK BREAST: Scoring helps release the
fat between the skin and the flesh. Using a chef's
knife, gently pierce the skin of the duck by just barely
grazing it (cutting about ¼ inch deep) from one edge
to the other. Score the skin in three consecutive spots
½ inch apart and again across the grain in three other
consecutive slices, creating a "grid" across the duck skin.

Don't have butcher's twine on hand? Use clean cotton twine from the hardware store, or you can even use toothpicks to pin those legs down. Don't let this chicken intimidate you—she's a beaut, but so are you!

whole roasted
go-to chicken

IF YOU MASTER ONLY TWO RECIPES in this book, it should be my Kale and Fennel Caesar on page 99 and this one. Dressed to kill with a garlic rub, stuffed with fresh aromatic herbs, this recipe is a knockout. Now you just need to worry about what to wear!

FWB: Chicken, garlic

Makes 6 servings

GARLIC BUTTER
¾ garlic head, peeled
¼ cup extra-virgin olive oil
3 fresh thyme sprigs, stems discarded
1 tablespoon butter, softened
¾ teaspoon sea salt

CHICKEN
1 (5-6 pounds) roasting chicken
1 teaspoon sea salt
½ lemon, thinly sliced into wheels
3 fresh thyme sprigs
2 fresh rosemary sprigs
1 garlic head, unpeeled, halved and broken into cloves

TO MAKE THE GARLIC BUTTER

In a food processor, combine all ingredients. Blend until a perfectly smooth paste forms.

TO MAKE THE CHICKEN

1 Preheat the oven to 400°F. With clean hands, wash the chicken, remove the giblets, and pat the chicken completely dry with paper towels.

2 Lightly grease the bottom of a sturdy roasting pan. Salt the inside of the chicken with 1 teaspoon sea salt and stuff with the lemon wheels, thyme, rosemary, and garlic.

3 Using butcher's twine, truss the chicken (breast side up), making sure to tuck in the wings and legs tightly. Place the chicken in the roasting pan and generously baste it with the garlic butter.

4 Cover the chicken loosely with aluminum foil and roast for approximately 2 hours. (Cook whole roasting chickens, fully thawed, 20 to 25 minutes per pound.) Remove the foil for the last 30 minutes of roasting time. Make sure the internal temperature reaches 165°F, the juices run clear, and the flesh is firm to the touch.

PER SERVING: 542 calories, 43 g fat (12 g saturated), 35 g protein, 0 g fiber, 0 g sugars, 838 mg sodium, 3 g carbohydrates

crispy lemongrass-pepper chicken

IF YOU'RE USED TO MAKING LEMON-PEPPER chicken, this recipe adds a little Asian twist that's sure to make your date sit up and take notice. With exotic lemongrass, fragrant sesame oil, and rice wine vinegar, plus mild, sweet honey and crisp cornflakes, this dish will leave you happy and satisfied, with zero guilt.

FWB: Chicken

Makes 4 servings

MARINADE

1 cup reduced-sodium soy sauce

½ cup rice wine vinegar

¼ teaspoon roasted sesame oil

2 tablespoons honey

3 tablespoons finely chopped lemongrass

CHICKEN

3 pounds boneless, skinless chicken breast and/or thighs

3 cups cornflakes

2 tablespoons finely chopped lemongrass

¾ teaspoons sea salt, divided

½ cup panko breadcrumbs

2 eggs, lightly beaten

¼ teaspoon black pepper

TO MAKE THE MARINADE

In a large bowl, whisk together all the ingredients for the marinade.

TO MAKE THE CHICKEN

1 Add the chicken to the marinade, making sure it is completely submerged for at least 3 hours, or overnight.

2 Preheat the oven to 400°F. Place a wire baking rack on top of a small baking sheet. Set aside.

3 In a food processor, combine the cornflakes and 2 tablespoons lemongrass. Process until finely crushed and well incorporated. Add ½ teaspoon of the salt and panko to this mixture and set aside.

4 Transfer the eggs to a shallow dish. Coat the marinated chicken pieces with the beaten eggs and dredge them in the cornflake mixture.

5 Place the chicken on the prepared baking rack. Bake until golden and crispy on all sides, about 30 to 40 minutes. Sprinkle with the remaining ¼ teaspoon sea salt and black pepper to finish.

PER SERVING: 405 calories, 13 g fat (3 g saturated), 51 g protein, 0 g fiber, 5 g sugars, 630 mg sodium, 18 g carbohydrates

the better burger and homemade quick pickles

YOU DIDN'T THINK I'D WRITE A cookbook without a burger recipe, did you? My secret to a sexier burger? Juicy, sweet caramelized onions and mouthwatering pickles.

FWB. Lean sirloin, onion

Makes 5 servings

QUICK PICKLES

2 pickling cucumbers, such as Kirby, cut into ¼-inch slices on a mandoline

1½ teaspoons sea salt

2 cups apple cider vinegar

1 cup light brown sugar

½ yellow onion, thinly sliced

2 garlic cloves, slivered

1 teaspoon dill seed

1 teaspoon mustard seed

1 teaspoon cumin seed

BURGERS

½ tablespoon unsalted butter

1 large yellow onion, halved and thinly sliced

¼ cup water

2 teaspoons sea salt, divided

1½ pounds 95% lean ground sirloin

¼ teaspoon black pepper

1 tablespoon extra-virgin olive oil

5 brioche buns or potato rolls, split and toasted (see tip)

8 leaves Bibb lettuce

1 ripe tomato, sliced

TO MAKE THE PICKLES

1 Place the cucumber slices in a colander set in the sink. Sprinkle them with the 1½ teaspoons salt and stir to combine. Let stand for 20 minutes. Rinse, drain, and transfer the cucumbers to a large heatproof bowl.

2 Meanwhile, combine the apple cider vinegar, brown sugar, onion, garlic, dill, mustard seed, and cumin seed in a medium saucepan. Bring to a boil.

3 Reduce the heat and simmer for 10 minutes. Pour the hot liquid over the cucumbers and stir to combine. Refrigerate for at least 10 minutes to bring to room temperature.

TO MAKE THE BURGERS

1 In a large skillet, melt the butter. Add the onion and cook over moderate heat, stirring occasionally, until deep golden, about 40 minutes. Add the water and scrape up any browned bits. Cook until the liquid evaporates, about 5 minutes. Season the caramelized onion with 1 teaspoon of the sea salt, and keep warm.

2 Meanwhile, season the sirloin generously with the remaining 1 teaspoon salt and the pepper. Gently shape the sirloin into five 1-inch-thick patties.

3 In a large cast-iron skillet, heat the oil. Cook the burgers over moderately high heat until deep brown outside and medium-rare within, about 6 minutes per side.

(continued)

4 Transfer the burgers to the buns, top with the caramelized onion, and serve with lettuce, tomato, and a side of
   your homemade quick pickles.

*For less sodium, use 1 teaspoon total instead of the
2 teaspoons sea salt called for in this recipe.*

PER SERVING: 460 calories, 15 g fat (6 g saturated), 38 g protein,
2 g fiber, 8 g sugars, 670 mg sodium, 40 g carbohydrates

BENEFIT THAT BOD: Want your burger and a skinny
waist, too? Make an open-faced burger by leaving off
the top bun and digging in with a knife or a fork. Or
just lose the bun altogether and serve the burger on
top of Bibb lettuce.

rosemary- and dijon-crusted pork tenderloin

LEAN AND FRAGRANT, PORK IS TRULY the new white meat. Crust up a tenderloin with fresh rosemary, garlic, and Dijon mustard and you've got a simple, budget-friendly baste-and-roast recipe that looks and tastes like a million bucks.

FWB: Lean pork, rosemary

Makes 6 servings

1 (1½–2 pounds) pork tenderloin
½ cup panko breadcrumbs
1 tablespoon finely chopped fresh rosemary
2 garlic cloves, minced
1 teaspoon sea salt
2 tablespoons Dijon mustard

1 Preheat the oven to 400°F. Line a baking sheet with aluminum foil. Coat lightly with cooking spray.

2 Rinse the pork tenderloin and pat it completely dry with paper towels.

3 In a small mixing bowl, mix the panko, rosemary, and garlic.

4 Season both sides of the pork tenderloin with the sea salt, and then generously brush the entire tenderloin with the Dijon.

5 Press the herbed panko mixture into the tenderloin to form a thick crust.

6 Roast the pork tenderloin in the oven for approximately 35 to 45 minutes, or until firm to the touch. Make sure that the internal temperature reaches 145°F.

7 Serve alongside the Homemade Apple Chutney on page 56.

PER SERVING: 149 calories, 3 g fat (1 g saturated), 24 g protein, 0 g fiber, 0 g sugars, 377 mg sodium, 5 g carbohydrates

KEEP IT FABULOUS: Love this recipe enough to try it twice? Go for the same ingredients, but change up the protein: Try a rack of lamb, pork chops, or even beef tenderloin.

marry me spaghetti and meatballs

WHEN MY PARENTS MET, IT WAS love at first sight. After moving to the United States from Japan in the 1970s, my mother nailed every American recipe! It's no wonder her spaghetti and meatballs was one of their favorite meals. They've been happily married for more than 30 years.

FWB: Lean pork and beef

Makes 6 servings (30 meatballs)

8 ounces 80% lean ground beef chuck

8 ounces lean ground pork

1 garlic clove, minced

¼ cup finely chopped fresh flat-leaf parsley

1 cup finely chopped cremini mushrooms (about 4 medium mushrooms)

1 large egg, lightly beaten

1 cup panko breadcrumbs

2 teaspoons sea salt

Candice's Homemade Marinara Sauce, page 133

1 tablespoon extra-virgin olive oil

1 box (14.5–16 ounces) whole wheat spaghetti

1 In a large mixing bowl, mix together the beef and pork, using your hands. Stir in the garlic, parsley, mushrooms, egg, panko, and sea salt. Lightly dampen your hands and roll the mixture into 1-inch balls, transferring them to a rimmed baking sheet as you work. Refrigerate for 1 hour.

2 Bring the sauce to a gentle simmer in a medium pot. Meanwhile, heat the oil in a heavy medium skillet over medium-high heat.

3 Working in batches, fry the meatballs, shaking the skillet occasionally, until they are brown all over, about 6 minutes. Transfer them to the sauce. Simmer until the meatballs are cooked through, about 10 minutes. (Test for doneness by cutting 1 meatball open.)

4 Bring a large pot of heavily salted water to a boil. Cook the spaghetti to al dente. Strain and run under cool water to stop the cooking.

5 Place the cooked spaghetti back in the large pot. Toss the cooked spaghetti with about 1 to 2 cups of Candice's Homemade Marinara Sauce to keep it from sticking together. Serve paired with some Cabernet and my Kale and Fennel Caesar on page 99. Serve extra marinara sauce at the table, if desired.

PER SERVING: 341 calories, 17 g fat (5 g saturated), 20 g protein, 3 g fiber, 12 g sugars, 909 mg sodium, 26 g carbohydrates

Spaghetti and meatballs doesn't have to be as naughty as you think. Lighten up the recipe by adding more chopped mushrooms, and pan-fry lightly, using half the oil and a nonstick pan. Make sure you limit the size and number of meatballs as well. Five 1-inch meatballs should serve you just fine!

oxtail ragu with pappardelle

THIS MAY BE ONE OF THE RICHEST, heartiest recipes in this entire book—and it's sure to please and satisfy any man's palate. Indulge with a great bottle of red wine and see where the night takes you.

FWB: Tomatoes, carrots

Makes 6 servings

3 tablespoons extra-virgin olive oil

2 pounds oxtail*

Sea salt to taste

1 yellow onion, finely chopped

3 carrots, finely diced

3 celery stalks, finely diced

3 bay leaves

5 thyme sprigs

6 garlic cloves, minced

1 (28-ounce) can organic diced tomatoes

1 cup high-quality dry red wine, such as Merlot or Chianti

1 (16-ounce) package pappardelle noodles

¼ cup part-skim ricotta cheese (optional)

Fresh basil

*Call your local butcher ahead of time to see if it is in stock.

1   Add the olive oil to a large stockpot over medium heat. Season the oxtail with sea salt and place it in the pot. Brown both sides, remove, and reserve.

2   Add the onion to the pot and reduce the heat to low. Cook for about 8 to 10 minutes. Add the carrots and celery, followed by the bay leaves, thyme, and garlic. Cook for another 15 minutes, or until the vegetables are soft and fragrant.

3   Add the tomatoes and wine and raise the heat to medium, stirring just to deglaze the bits on the bottom. Return the oxtail to the pot. Place a lid on the pot and bring to a slow boil. Immediately turn down the heat to medium-low and cook gently for 3 to 4 hours. You will notice the meat melting from the bone and a delicious layer of fat melting into the sauce.

4   Using tongs, remove the oxtail from the pot. When cool to the touch, pick off any meat that is still attached to the bone. Place the meat back in the pot and discard the bones. Season the sauce with salt to taste.

5   Cook the noodles according to the package directions, strain, and shock with cold water. Using tongs, place the noodles in the ragu and gently toss to coat. Serve with a dollop of part-skim ricotta, if desired, and fresh basil.

PER SERVING: 551 calories, 14 g fat (4 g saturated), 25 g protein, 5 g fiber, 7 g sugars, 448 mg sodium, 73 g carbohydrates

orecchiette with broccoli raab and sun-dried tomato pesto

THIS RECIPE IS GREAT FOR A sexy, fun, hands-on date night. Cook it together, and then savor every bite, along with a light Pinot Noir or a classic Chianti.

FWB: Almonds, broccoli raab

Makes 4 servings

HOMEMADE ORECCHIETTE

2 cups all-purpose flour

1 cup semolina flour

½ teaspoon sea salt, or to taste

¾ cup warm water, or more or less depending on dough consistency

1 tablespoon extra-virgin olive oil

SUN-DRIED TOMATO PESTO

2 cups fresh basil

½ cup raw almonds

½ teaspoon sea salt

½ cup extra-virgin olive oil

1 tablespoon lemon juice

½ cup sun-dried tomatoes, strained (if oil packed)

1 garlic clove

BROCCOLI RAAB

1 tablespoon extra-virgin olive oil

2 teaspoons minced garlic

1 bunch broccoli raab, chopped, tough stems removed

½ teaspoon chili flakes

Parmesan cheese (optional)

Finishing salt (optional)

TO MAKE THE DOUGH

1 On a clean work surface, combine the all-purpose flour, semolina flour, and sea salt. Make a well in the center of the flour and add approximately ¼ cup of warm water. Using a fork, working from the inside in a circular motion, begin to incorporate the flour and liquid. Continue adding water until a dough forms. Knead well on a lightly floured board until the dough is smooth and elastic. This may take 20 minutes or so.

2 Form the dough into a ball, wrap it with plastic, and place it in the fridge to firm up for at least 1 hour.

TO MAKE THE PESTO

Place all the ingredients in a food processor and blend well! Add more or less olive oil, lemon juice, garlic, and so on to taste.

TO MAKE THE ORECCHIETTE

1 Pull off a scant handful of the dough, keeping the rest of the dough covered. On a lightly floured board, roll the dough into a rope about ¾ inch in diameter.

2 Cut the rope into slices no more than ⅛ inch thick to form small circles of dough. Put one of these circles into the cupped palm of your hand and, with the thumb of the other hand, press and turn the circle at the same time to form a dent in the center that will spread the

(continued)

dough a little on each side. It should look like a small ear, with slightly thicker earlobes. Repeat with all of the remaining dough, placing the orecchiette on a lightly floured cloth as they are made.

TO MAKE THE BROCCOLI RAAB

Heat 1 tablespoon olive oil in a medium sauté pan. Add the garlic and broccoli raab and cook until tender, approximately 6 minutes. Finish by sprinkling with the chili flakes. Add sea salt as needed. Set aside.

TO FINISH

1 Bring a large pot of salted water to a boil. Cook the orecchiette until they float to the surface, approximately 4 minutes. Use a spider or slotted spoon to transfer the orecchiette to a large bowl.

2 Toss the pasta with the pesto to coat and add the sautéed broccoli raab. Serve with a sprinkle of Parmesan or finishing salt, such as Maldon, if desired.

PER SERVING: 830 calories, 46 g fat (6 g saturated), 19 g protein, 7 g fiber, 5 g sugars, 556 mg sodium, 90 g carbohydrates

KEEP IT SEXY: Want to impress your date even more? Have the ingredients on hand to prepare my Port-Soaked Cherry and Dark Chocolate Brownies on page 229. Save some of the port wine from the recipe to drink with dessert. Warning: This may lead to an over-the-top makeout session!

sunnyside stuffed baked potatoes

EGGS ARE AN INEXPENSIVE, HIGH-QUALITY, LEAN protein that you can consume at any meal. I prefer Eggland's Best eggs, with more omega-3s and lutein and less saturated fat. Or look for organic eggs from chickens fed with vegetarian feed.

FWB: Spinach, eggs

Makes 4 servings

4 large russet potatoes
1 tablespoon extra-virgin olive oil
1 small yellow onion, finely chopped
1 cup baby bella mushrooms, thinly sliced
1½ teaspoons sea salt, divided
2 cups chopped spinach or baby spinach
4 large eggs
1 teaspoon fennel seeds
¼ teaspoon black pepper

1 Preheat the oven to 400°F. Scrub the skin of the potatoes and pat dry with paper towels. Using a fork, poke 5 holes in each potato and bake until fork-tender, about 1 hour.

2 Heat the olive oil in a medium skillet over medium heat. Add the onion and cook for 8 minutes, until fragrant. Lower the heat, then add the mushrooms and 1 teaspoon of the sea salt. Cook for 5 minutes, or until the mushrooms are fragrant and soft. Toss in the spinach and cook just until wilted, about 2 minutes.

3 Heat a separate nonstick skillet over medium heat. Lightly coat the skillet with cooking spray and begin to cook the eggs. After 2 minutes, sprinkle the eggs with fennel seeds, the remaining ½ teaspoon sea salt, and the pepper, and cook until the yolk is medium and still slightly runny.

4 Cut a horizontal slit in the top of each potato, about 3 inches deep and 4 to 5 inches long. Open up the potato by gently pushing out its sides. Stuff the opening with the spinach/mushroom mixture. Gently place an egg on top of each potato.

PER SERVING: 412 calories, 9 g fat (2 g saturated), 15 g protein, 6 g fiber, 4 g sugars, 448 mg sodium, 71 g carbohydrates

"When baking, follow directions.
When cooking,
go by your own taste."
Laiko Bahrs

CHAPTER 13

Sultry Sweets and Splurges

Ever since I was a li'l munchkin, I've had a major sweet tooth for all kinds of cakes, cookies, and sugary treats. But I've learned how to eat dessert in moderation and have come up with my own recipes to save calories without sacrificing sweet goodness. I still can't resist my homemade Cornflake–Chocolate Chip Cookies (I always have a stash in my freezer), and I keep an emergency supply of Cherry-Pistachio Biscotti in my pantry. Of course you don't have to say good-bye to dessert to stay sexy! You simply have to learn a few of my secret swaps and satisfying tips.

blueberry-lime spelt cake

I CHALLENGE YOU TO TRY SPELT FLOUR! It has a rich, nutty taste, and it's easier for your body to digest than wheat flour. Plus, with bennies like vitamin B_2, copper, protein, and fiber, it's a win-win choice. Jackpot!

FWB: Oats, spelt

Makes 16 servings

OATMEAL CRUMBLE TOPPING

1 cup organic rolled oats

1 tablespoon sugar

½ teaspoon ground cinnamon

½ teaspoon ground nutmeg

2 egg whites

2 tablespoons butter, cut into small cubes

CAKE

1½ cups fresh or frozen blueberries, rinsed (if using frozen, toss with 2 tablespoons flour)

2 tablespoons all-purpose flour

2¼ cups spelt flour

1 teaspoon baking soda

1 teaspoon aluminum-free baking powder

¼ teaspoon sea salt

3 eggs

⅔ cup sugar

1 cup ripe mashed banana

3 tablespoons butter, melted

1 teaspoon vanilla extract

¾ cup low-fat buttermilk

Zest and juice of 1 whole lime

TO MAKE THE TOPPING

In a small bowl, combine all the ingredients for the topping. Make sure to incorporate the butter cubes evenly into the crumble. Set aside.

TO MAKE THE CAKE

1 Preheat the oven to 325°F. Lightly grease a 9-inch × 9-inch baking pan and line it with parchment paper.

2 In a separate small bowl, toss together the blueberries and all-purpose flour. Set aside.

3 In a medium bowl, whisk together the spelt flour, baking soda, baking powder, and sea salt.

4 In a large bowl, whisk the eggs and sugar together until well blended and creamy.

5 In a separate bowl, blend the mashed banana with the melted butter. Whisk until light and fluffy, making sure that there are no banana chunks remaining. Mix into the egg and sugar mixture, and then add the vanilla, buttermilk, and lime zest and juice. Gradually add the flour mixture to the wet ingredients, stirring to incorporate after each addition.

6 Gently fold in the blueberries. Fill the pan with the cake batter.

7 Spread the reserved crumble topping evenly over the cake.

(continued)

8 Bake until a toothpick inserted into the center of the cake comes out clean, approximately 1 hour 15 minutes.

9 Remove from the oven and let the cake cool slightly in the pan, then remove it from the pan and finish cooling on a rack.

PER SERVING: 190 calories, 5 g fat (3 g saturated), 5 g protein, 2 g fiber, 14 g sugars, 202 mg sodium, 32 g carbohydrates

For ease of mashing, microwave the banana and butter mixture together for about 10 to 15 seconds to make it softer and easier to whisk.

creamy coconut–
black rice pudding

THIS CREAMY RECIPE IS AN EXOTIC, luscious twist on rice pudding. It's perfect for a date night in, and it's incredibly easy to make. It will surprise you in every good way!

FWB: Ginger

Makes 12 servings

2 cups black rice (not wild rice)

5 cups water

Pinch of sea salt

¾ cup sugar

1 (13.5–15-ounce) can light coconut milk

1–2 teaspoons finely grated fresh ginger

1 stalk lemongrass (optional)

1 In a large saucepan, bring the rice, water, and sea salt to a boil. Then reduce the heat to low and simmer for approximately 45 minutes.

2 Stir in the sugar, coconut milk, ginger, and lemongrass (if using), and gently bring to a light boil. Reduce the heat to low and simmer, uncovered, while stirring occasionally, until the mixture has thickened.

3 Remove from the heat and cool to room temperature. Stir the pudding before serving. Serve topped with some fresh grated ginger or even a surprising sweet treat, like the Cinnamon-Sugar Baked Sweet Potatoes on page 147.

PER SERVING: 185 calories, 3 g fat (2 g saturated), 4 g protein, 2 g fiber, 13 g sugars, 37 mg sodium, 38 g carbohydrates

size zero cake

WHO SAYS YOU CAN STUFF YOUR FACE with birthday cake only once a year? With this Size Zero Cake, you won't feel an ounce of guilt following any celebration. Pop that Champagne, enjoy the company of friends and family, and make a wish. Here's to a cake that begs for seconds, without a second on your hips—and may all the rest of your dreams come true!

FWB: Bananas, almond milk

Makes 16 servings

CAKE

1 medium, very ripe banana

2 cups cake flour

1 cup all-purpose flour

1 teaspoon baking soda

1 teaspoon aluminum-free baking powder

¼ teaspoon sea salt

⅓ cup butter, softened

1½ cups sugar

3 large eggs

1 teaspoon organic vanilla extract

1½ cups buttermilk

CHOCOLATE HAZELNUT FROSTING

⅓ cup + 2 tablespoons unsweetened almond milk, as needed

2 tablespoons chocolate hazelnut butter (such as Justin's)

¾ cup high-quality unsweetened cocoa powder

3 cups confectioners' sugar

TO MAKE THE CAKE

1 Preheat the oven to 350°F. Lightly grease and flour two 8-inch round cake pans.

2 In a small bowl, mash the banana.

3 In a medium bowl, mix the cake flour, all-purpose flour, baking soda, baking powder, and sea salt. Set aside.

4 In a large bowl, cream the butter and sugar until light and fluffy. Beat in the eggs, one at a time. Add the vanilla.

5 Gently fold in the mashed banana.

6 Gently whisk in the flour mixture, while alternating with the buttermilk.

7 Pour the batter into the pans and bake for 35 to 45 minutes, or until the top of the cake is a light golden brown and firm to the touch.*

TO MAKE THE FROSTING

1 In a large mixing bowl, using an electric mixer, combine ¼ cup almond milk with the chocolate hazelnut butter until smooth.

2 In a separate bowl, sift together the cocoa powder and confectioners' sugar.

(continued)

3　Slowly incorporate the sifted dry ingredients into the hazelnut butter mixture in small batches, alternating the dry ingredients with the remaining almond milk until well combined. The frosting will reach a firm but smooth consistency.

4　Allow the cake to cool prior to frosting. Start with the bottom layer on a cake stand or serving platter. Stack the second layer directly on top and frost, coating the entire top and sides of the cake. Decorate as desired and serve up a slice of that Size Zero!

While the cake is baking, prepare the chocolate hazelnut frosting.

PER SERVING: 339 calories, 7 g fat (3.5 g saturated), 5 g protein, 2 g fiber, 44 g sugars, 227 mg sodium, 67 g carbohydrates

KEEP IT FABULOUS: Don't have any fancy sprinkles or cake decor on hand? Crush up some hazelnuts, or add sliced almonds on top of this beautiful cake. Zest an orange or sprinkle the rim of the cake with some confectioners' sugar for a sexy yet slimming treat.

cherry-pistachio biscotti

ONCE YOU MAKE THESE LITTLE LOGS of love, you will see how simple and easy they are. Simply mix the batter, shape, and bake. You'll be shocked at how delicious good fat (extra-virgin olive oil) tastes.

FWB: Cherries, pistachios

Makes 2 dozen

¼ cup extra virgin olive oil

½ cup brown sugar

1 teaspoon vanilla extract

2 eggs

1¾ cups all-purpose flour

½ teaspoon sea salt

1 teaspoon aluminum-free baking powder

1½ cups raw pistachios, coarsely chopped

2 cups pitted cherries, halved and coarsely chopped (if using frozen, do not thaw; discard liquid and toss in 1 tablespoon all-purpose flour)

1 Preheat the oven to 350°F.

2 In a large mixing bowl, combine the oil and sugar until well blended. Mix in the vanilla extract, then beat in the eggs. Combine the flour, sea salt, and baking powder; gradually stir into the egg mixture. Using a spatula, gently mix in the pistachios and cherries.

3 Lightly flour your hands and a work surface. Divide the dough in half and shape it into two 10-inch × 2-inch logs on a baking sheet lined with foil. If your dough is sticky, lightly flour your hands again.

4 Bake for 40 to 45 minutes, or just until the logs are light brown and slightly firm on top. Remove from the oven and set aside to cool for 10 minutes.

5 Reduce the oven temperature to 275°F. Remove the logs from the baking sheet, and, using a serrated knife, cut the logs on a diagonal into ¾-inch-thick slices. Lay them on their sides on the same baking sheet. Bake approximately 45 to 50 more minutes (turning halfway through), or until dry and firm to the touch. Cool and serve with some hazelnut coffee or a spot of English Breakfast tea.

PER SERVING. 124 calories, 6 g fat (1 g saturated), 3 g protein, 1 g fiber, 5 g sugars, 80 mg sodium, 14 g carbohydrates

KEEP IT FABULOUS: Biscotti are a great little treat and a perfect gift. Wrap them up in little cellophane bags and tie with a bow. See page 225 for a holiday version.

cornflake–chocolate chip cookies

AFTER VISITING THE FAMED MOMOFUKU MILK BAR in NYC, I fell in love—with my favorite new cookie. I had to create my own recipe, and my secret swap of mashed banana for butter guarantees a guilt-free version. These chewy, delightful bites are now a staple in my freezer. Enjoy!

FWB: Bananas, eggs

Makes 2 dozen

3 tablespoons butter, at room temperature

½ cup mashed banana

1 cup packed brown sugar

1 teaspoon vanilla extract

2 eggs

1 cup all-purpose flour

1 teaspoon baking soda

1 teaspoon aluminum-free baking powder

½ teaspoon sea salt

½ teaspoon ground cinnamon

1 cup semisweet chocolate chips

3 cups cornflakes, crushed (preferably organic)

2 tablespoons shredded sweetened coconut (optional)

1 Preheat the oven to 350°F. Line a baking sheet with foil and spray it with cooking spray.

2 Whisk together the butter, mashed banana, brown sugar, and vanilla until creamy and fluffy.

3 Add the 2 eggs and whisk well to combine.

4 In a separate bowl, gently sift together the flour, baking soda, baking powder, sea salt, and cinnamon.

5 Gently sift the dry ingredients into the wet ingredients, whisking to incorporate.

6 Lightly fold in the chocolate chips, cornflakes, and coconut, if desired.

7 Using a small ice cream scoop, place the cookies on the baking sheet, leaving 1½ inches between cookies.

8 Bake for 12 to 15 minutes. Refrigerate the remaining dough while you are baking the first batch. Repeat with the second batch.

PER SERVING: 124 calories, 4 g fat (2 g saturated), 2 g protein, 1 g fiber, 14 g sugars, 161 mg sodium, 22 g carbohydrates

I don't recommend that you store this dough overnight, since the cornflakes will get mushy. If you need to store it for the next day, simply add the cornflakes just before baking.

lavender sugar rose petals

THIS IS A SIMPLE AND LOVELY garnish to top your favorite cakes, cupcakes, or even French toast. This amazing batch of edible rose petals will be your new go-to when you're in need of a loving touch for any sweet treat!

Makes 1 dozen

2 large egg whites
12 organic/unsprayed rose petals
½ cup Lavender Rose Petal Sugar
   (page 32)

1 Whisk the egg whites gently with a fork. Carefully pick up a rose petal.

2 Lightly brush both sides of the petal with the egg whites. Sprinkle the petal with the Lavender Rose Petal Sugar.

3 Transfer to a cooling rack to dry. Repeat with all the rose petals. Store in an airtight container for up to a week.

PER SERVING (1 PETAL): 35 calories, 0 g fat (0 g saturated), 1 g protein, 0 g fiber, 8 g sugars, 9 mg sodium, 8 g carbohydrates

Definitely make sure that your roses are organic and never sprayed with chemicals before you pluck them. Ask Mom if you can raid her garden (thanks, Mom!).

quinoa–peanut butter–granola bars

AFTER MAKING A BATCH OF THESE BARS as a thank-you treat for a crew out in LA after a long shoot, they begged for the recipe. Well, here you have it! Without preservatives, icky fake fillers, or processed chemicals, these are feel-good granola bars all the way!

FWB: Quinoa, almonds

Makes 20 small bars

2 cups organic rolled oats

2 cups quinoa flakes (check at your local health food store)

1 cup raw almonds

½ cup unsweetened dry coconut

¼ cup sesame seeds

¼ cup flaxseed

1 cup honey

1¾ cups natural peanut butter

½ teaspoon ground cinnamon

½ teaspoon sea salt

2 cups chopped dried fruit (cranberries, apricots, pineapple, currants, cherries–your choice!)

1 Spray or lightly butter a 13-inch × 9-inch baking dish and line it with parchment paper or aluminum foil. Preheat the oven to 350°F.

2 Spread the oats, quinoa flakes, and almonds over a baking sheet. Place it in the oven and toast for 10 minutes, stirring occasionally. Add the coconut, sesame seeds, and flaxseed and toast for another 2 minutes.

3 In the meantime, combine the honey, peanut butter, cinnamon, and sea salt in a medium saucepan and place it over medium heat. Cook until everything is combined.

4 Once the oat mixture is toasted, remove it from the oven and immediately add it to the liquid mixture. Add the dried fruit, and mix everything together to coat evenly.

5 Turn the mixture out into the prepared baking dish and press down, evenly distributing the mixture in the dish.

6 Let cool, then cut into squares and store in an airtight container for up to a week.

PER SERVING: 381 calories, 19 g fat (4 g saturated), 11 g protein, 7 g fiber, 26 g sugars, 170 mg sodium, 46 g carbohydrates

KEEP IT FABULOUS: If you don't have quinoa flakes on hand, opt for half oatmeal, half bran flakes, or even a cup of crispy rice cereal.

sweet peach cobbler

THERE'S SOMETHING JUST SO COMFORTING ABOUT fresh peach cobbler! Combine the tartness of fresh peaches and the nutritional goodness from the organic oats, and you can't go wrong. With half the fat and calories of a regular cobbler, this recipe is definitely feel-good food.

FWB: Peaches, oats

Makes 8 servings

PEACH FILLING

½ cup granulated sugar

¼ teaspoon ground cinnamon

¼ teaspoon ground nutmeg

5–6 cups fresh or frozen and thawed peeled, pitted, and sliced peaches

2 tablespoons lemon juice

OAT TOPPING

½ cup all-purpose flour

½ teaspoon baking soda

½ teaspoon aluminum-free baking powder

¼ teaspoon sea salt

2 tablespoons butter, softened

½ cup brown sugar, firmly packed

1 egg

1 teaspoon vanilla extract

¼ cup water

1½ cups organic rolled oats

TO MAKE THE FILLING

1 In a large saucepan, combine the sugar, cinnamon, and nutmeg. Stir in the peaches and lemon juice, tossing until the peaches are evenly coated.

2 Cook the peach filling over medium heat, stirring constantly, until the mixture begins to thicken. Pour the peach filling into an ungreased 8-inch × 8-inch baking dish.

TO MAKE THE TOPPING

1 Preheat the oven to 350°F.

2 In a medium mixing bowl, whisk together the flour, baking soda, baking powder, and sea salt.

3 In an additional medium mixing bowl, blend the butter, brown sugar, egg, and vanilla. Add the water and whisk well, until fluffy and the color lightens. Stir the flour mixture into the creamed mixture until no flour is visible. Stir in the oats until just incorporated.

4 Using a large spoon, drop the oat crumble mix onto the peach mixture. Bake for 30 to 40 minutes, or until the topping is golden brown.

PER SERVING: 265 calories, 5 g fat (2 g saturated), 5 g protein, 3 g fiber, 34 g sugars, 219 mg sodium, 52 g carbohydrates

KEEP IT FABULOUS: Top off this cobbler with 0% Greek yogurt, candied walnuts, or candied pecans. Enjoy with a glass of Sancerre or sparkling white wine.

classic caramel apples with lavender rose petal sugar and coconut

ONE BITE OF THESE APPLES AND I'm right back at the good ol' Del Mar Fair in San Diego. As kids, we all loved these caramel confections. I like to pass these out at birthdays and showers and watch the smiles light up the room.

FWB: Apples

Makes 6 servings

6 small Granny Smith apples, about 2–2½ inches in diameter (you can use any variety, but Granny seems to hold up the best and is the tartest)

¾ cup sugar

¼ cup light corn syrup

2 tablespoons water

3 tablespoons butter

3 tablespoons heavy whipping cream

OPTIONAL TOPPINGS
Lavender Rose Petal Sugar (page 32)
Lightly fluffed coconut shavings
Fine sea salt

1 Wash and thoroughly dry each apple. Remove the stems and place a stick in each resulting hole. Line a baking sheet with parchment and lightly coat it with cooking spray. Place all your toppings in shallow plates.

2 Premeasure all the ingredients. In a medium saucepan, combine the sugar, corn syrup, and water. Cook over medium heat until the sugar is completely dissolved. Bring to a boil over medium-high heat, stirring occasionally with a whisk or an oiled rubber spatula.

3 When the liquid-sugar mixture becomes a deep, golden brown, remove it from the heat and slowly add the butter and all of the cream, stirring constantly for 15 to 20 minutes.

4 Return to the heat, insert a candy thermometer, and continue cooking until the thermometer reads 230°F.

5 Remove from the heat and cool to 215°F, stirring occasionally. Working quickly, dip each apple into the caramel mixture until it is three-quarters coated, then immediately dip the bottom of the apple in the desired toppings. Place on the parchment-lined baking sheet to set. Store at room temperature for approximately 2 days.

PER SERVING: 268 calories, 9 g fat (5 g saturated), 0 g protein, 2 g fiber, 40 g sugars, 54 mg sodium, 51 g carbohydrates

cherry-pistachio clafoutis

CLAFOUTIS **IS FRENCH FOR "TO FILL."** This treat comes from the Limousin region of France. Both Nate Berkus and I agree this plain ol' pancake has the fanciest name around. Serve it up, and your guests will think you're fancy too. Enjoy on a relaxing Sunday morning with a cup of tea or coffee.

FWB: Cherries, pistachios

Makes 10 servings

1 tablespoon butter

1 tablespoon + ¾ cup all-purpose flour, divided

1 tablespoon vanilla extract

3 eggs

⅓ cup granulated sugar

1 cup half-and-half

½ teaspoon ground nutmeg

¼ teaspoon sea salt

¼ cup crushed pistachios, coarsly chopped

2 tablespoons elderflower cordial (optional)

1½ cups black cherries, halved and pitted

2 tablespoons confectioners' sugar (optional)

1 Preheat the oven to 425°F. Use the butter and 1 table-spoon of the flour to generously coat a 9-inch cast-iron skillet or baking dish.

2 In a large bowl, combine the vanilla extract, eggs, sugar, half-and-half, nutmeg, and sea salt. Using a whisk, blend for a few seconds to mix the ingredients, then add the remaining ¾ cup flour and whisk until smooth. Gently fold in the pistachios. Add the elder-flower cordial, if using.

3 Distribute the cherries evenly over the bottom of the skillet or baking dish, then pour the batter over the top.

4 Bake until a skewer inserted into the batter comes out clean and a golden brown crust has formed on the top and bottom of the clafoutis, about 30 minutes.

5 Allow the clafoutis to cool slightly, then add a dusting of confectioners' sugar, if desired.

PER SERVING: 169 calories, 7 g fat (3 g saturated), 5 g protein, 1 g fiber, 12 g sugars, 100 mg sodium, 22 g carbohydrates

This large, delicious pancake dream bakes up, rises fast, then falls! Make sure to pop it in the oven just before you serve it. It's prettiest when all puffed up and beautiful. You can bake it inside a reusable pie tin as well.

coconut-mango pops

IF YOU HAVEN'T COOKED WITH COCONUT milk before, this recipe offers an easy and delightful way to experiment! The exotic, creamy, rich coconut flavor will make you feel as though you're being whisked away to the tropics. Serve these pops on the next sweltering summer day and your friends will love you forever.

FWB: Mango

Makes 8 servings

2 cups frozen mango chunks

1 (13.6 ounce) can light coconut milk

2 tablespoons granulated sugar + more to taste

1 tablespoon lime juice

2 tablespoons shredded sweetened coconut (optional)

1 In a food processor, pulse the mango chunks, coconut milk, 2 tablespoons sugar, and lime juice until smooth. Stir in the shredded coconut, if using. Add additional sugar to taste.

2 Pour into frozen pop molds. Freeze for approximately 3 hours, or until the pops are solidified and can easily be removed from the molds.

PER SERVING: 73 calories, 2.7 g fat (2.4 g saturated), 1 g protein, 1 g fiber, 11 g sugars, 9 mg sodium, 11 g carbohydrates

Having a hard time removing your pops? Run the molds under warm water for easy release.

faux peanut butter–banana ice cream

IF YOU'RE ANYTHING LIKE ME, YOU'RE obsessed with spooning—not just with a loved one but with anything sweet and creamy! However, too many spoonfuls can cost you your waistline. Here's my favorite guiltless recipe to spoon away and enjoy a satisfying cold treat.

FWB: Bananas, peanut butter

Makes 4 servings

3 frozen bananas, peeled and sliced into chunks

¼ cup unsweetened almond milk

2 tablespoons natural peanut butter

1 teaspoon honey

Dark chocolate chips or shavings (optional)

1 Blend the banana chunks, almond milk, peanut butter, and honey in a food processor for 30 seconds, or until smooth.

2 Serve and garnish with your favorite brand of dark chocolate chips or shavings, if desired. Store in an airtight container in the freezer for the perfect dessert or late night snack! Mmmm.

PER SERVING: 132 calories, 4 g fat (1 g saturated), 3 g protein, 3 g fiber, 13 g sugars, 50 mg sodium, 23 g carbohydrates

This recipe contains less than half the fat of regular lactose-filled ice cream, creating a perfect guilt-free moment of bliss for your vegan and lactose-intolerant friends.

light pineapple upside-down cake

I WROTE THIS RECIPE AS AN "aloha" to my Hawaiian family—it's light, simple, and delicious! Hawaii has the most amazing pineapples in sight, the freshest ingredients, and all the love in the world. This cake was developed in the Aloha State, and I savor each bite as a little trip back there!

FWB: Pineapple

Makes 15 servings

⅔ cup pineapple juice, reserved from the can

½ cup packed brown sugar

1½ teaspoons butter

1 (20-ounce) can pineapple slices, drained, juice reserved (or 6 or 7 fresh pineapple rings)

¾ cup sugar

2 large eggs

1 teaspoon organic vanilla extract

2 cups all-purpose flour

½ teaspoon baking powder

½ teaspoon baking soda

½ teaspoon sea salt

½ teaspoon ground cinnamon

½ teaspoon ground nutmeg

1 cup low-fat buttermilk

½ cup crushed pineapple

1 Preheat the oven to 350°F. In a medium saucepan over medium heat, heat the pineapple juice and stir in the brown sugar. Whisk well to combine. Reduce the heat to low and reduce to a thickened, slightly syruplike consistency. Remove from the heat and set aside.

2 Use the butter to grease the bottom of a 10-inch skillet or 9-inch round cake pan. Arrange the pineapple rings in a single layer on the bottom of the pan, over the butter.

3 In a large bowl, cream the sugar and eggs until light and fluffy. Add the vanilla. Slowly add the flour, baking powder, baking soda, salt, cinnamon, and nutmeg, alternating with the buttermilk. Gently fold in crushed pineapple. Carefully pour the pineapple syrup over the pineapple in the skillet or pan.

4 Finally, pour the cake batter over the pineapple and syrup. Bake for 38 to 40 minutes. Insert a toothpick in the center of the cake and check if it comes out clean.

5 To serve, carefully invert the cake over your serving platter and serve warm with a side of fresh pitted cherries or topped with some toasted coconut, if desired.

PER SERVING: 190 calories, 1 g fat (0.5 g saturated), 3 g protein, 1 g fiber, 27 g sugars, 172 mg sodium, 41 g carbohydrates

"Biochemically, love is just like eating large amounts of chocolate."

John Milton

CHAPTER 14

Just Chocolate
(Need I Say More?)

Dear Chocolate: You are by far

the sexiest food of them all. Chocolate, if you were a man, you'd be David Beckham, Brad Pitt, and Pharrell Williams all melted into one big bite! There's nothing more perfect, sensual, and satisfying. It's no wonder I had to dedicate an entire chapter just to you. You thrill me even on my worst days. Our love story continues as I bake, whip, whisk, and melt you.

XOX,
CK

dark chocolate–orange cake

FEW THINGS IN THIS WORLD WILL put me into a quiet, Zen-like state. A great yoga class, acupuncture, or a food coma by chocolate will do just that. I've slashed some calories, tested the finest chocolates, and baked this one to perfection. Enjoy one of life's greatest pleasures, the flourless chocolate cake—with even less guilt!

FWB: Dark chocolate, cocoa powder

Makes 10 to 12 servings

CAKE

12 ounces high-quality premium dark chocolate, chopped

½ cup butter

5 eggs

¾ cup granulated sugar

¾ cup high-quality unsweetened cocoa powder

Zest of 1½ oranges (3–4 tablespoons)

DARK CHOCOLATE GANACHE

¾ cup heavy cream

1 cup finely chopped premium dark (70% cacao) chocolate

1 tablespoon Grand Marnier (optional)

TO MAKE THE CAKE

1 Preheat the oven to 325°F. Spray an 8-inch round spring-form pan with cooking spray and dust it with cocoa powder or a light coat of flour.

2 Make a double boiler: Bring a small pot of water to a simmer. Place a nonreactive bowl on top of the pot, making sure the bowl doesn't touch the water. Place the dark chocolate and butter in the bowl to melt. Gently mix them to combine with a rubber spatula. Remove from heat.

3 Whisk the eggs together in a separate bowl.

4 Stir in the sugar and cocoa powder. Mix gently. Let cool slightly and add the whisked eggs and orange zest, and stir until combined. Pour into the prepared pan.

5 Bake on the middle oven rack for 35 to 40 minutes, or until a toothpick inserted in the center comes out clean.

6 Remove from the oven and cool in the pan for 10 minutes, then turn out onto a wire rack to cool completely.

TO MAKE THE GANACHE

1 While the cake is baking, in a small saucepan, bring the heavy cream just to a boil. Have the chopped chocolate at hand in a bowl.

(continued)

2 Remove the hot cream from the heat and pour it over the chopped chocolate, mixing well to incorporate. Add the Grand Marnier, if desired.

3 Place the cooled cake on a mini rack on top of a baking sheet lined with parchment paper (to catch any excess chocolate ganache).

4 Pour the ganache to coat the entire Dark Chocolate Orange Cake. Chill until set.

PER SERVING: 444 calories, 33 g fat (19 g saturated), 8 g protein, 6 g fiber, 27 g sugars, 96 mg sodium, 37 g carbohydrates

double dark chocolate–mint biscotti

MINT AND CHOCOLATE IS ONE OF my favorite combos. Serve these up with hazelnut-infused coffee or hot cocoa for a toasty yet refreshing holiday treat.

FWB: Chocolate

Makes 2 dozen

1 cup all-purpose flour

½ teaspoon baking soda

⅓ cup high-quality unsweetened dark cocoa powder

¼ teaspoon sea salt

½ cup packed brown sugar

1 large egg

1 teaspoon peppermint or mint extract

¾ cup dark chocolate chips

¾ cup raw almonds (optional)

1 Preheat the oven to 350°F. In a large mixing bowl, add the flour, baking soda, cocoa powder, and sea salt, stirring with a whisk.

2 Combine the brown sugar, egg, and water in a separate bowl and beat with a mixer at high speed for 2 minutes. Add the peppermint extract and mix well.

3 Gently add the flour mixture into the egg mixture and stir until combined. Fold in the chocolate chips and almonds, if using.

4 Divide the dough into three equal portions. Lightly flour your hands and a work surface and roll each portion into a 6-inch-long roll. Place the logs on a baking sheet lined with foil. If your dough is sticky, lightly flour your hands again.

5 Bake for 35 to 40 minutes, or just until the logs are light brown and slightly firm on top. Remove from the oven and set aside to cool for approximately 10 minutes. Reduce the oven temperature to 275°F.

6 Remove the logs from the baking sheet, and, using a serrated knife, cut each log on a diagonal into eight ¾-inch-thick slices, creating a biscotti shape. Lay them on their sides back on the foil-lined baking sheet. Bake about 20 more minutes, or until dry and firm to the touch. Cool and serve or package.

PER SERVING: 82 calories, 3 g fat (2 g saturated), 2 g protein, 1 g fiber, 8 g sugars, 55 mg sodium, 14 g carbohydrates

Make a big batch of these cupcakes, save them in well-sealed containers, and freeze them until the next festive occasion. When ready to use, thaw at room temperature, and add the frosting. Easy!

mini chocolate and peanut butter cupcakes

SOME THINGS IN LIFE YOU MUST say yes to. You'll love these light mini cupcake bites, with a hint of coffee for a deep, dark, mochalike flavor. This is heaven, and with one-third fewer calories than in similar recipes!

FWB: Bananas, peanut butter

Makes 50

CUPCAKES

1 cup all-purpose flour

¾ cup high-quality unsweetened cocoa powder

1 teaspoon baking soda

½ teaspoon aluminum-free baking powder

½ teaspoon sea salt

¼ cup unsalted butter, at room temperature

½ large ripe banana, mashed (about ½ cup)

½ cup granulated sugar

½ cup packed light brown sugar

1 egg

1 teaspoon vanilla extract

1 cup strong coffee, chilled

½ cup mini dark chocolate chips

FROSTING

3 tablespoons natural peanut butter

5 cups confectioners' sugar

¼ cup + 3 tablespoons unsweetened almond milk

½ teaspoon vanilla extract

TO MAKE THE CUPCAKES

1 Preheat the oven to 350°F. Lightly grease a mini-cupcake tin or insert paper mini-cupcake liners.

2 Sift together the flour, cocoa, baking soda, baking powder, and sea salt. Set aside.

3 In a medium bowl, cream the butter, mashed banana, and sugars until light and fluffy. Add the egg and vanilla and beat well.

4 Alternately add the flour mixture and coffee to the creamed ingredients in three additions, beating until just incorporated. Fold in the chocolate chips.

5 Fill each muffin cup halfway with batter. (I love using my mini ice cream scoop here!) Bake for 10 to 12 minutes, or until a toothpick inserted into a cupcake comes out clean.

TO MAKE THE FROSTING

1 Meanwhile, in a small bowl, combine all the ingredients for the frosting. Using a hand mixer, blend until thoroughly combined. The frosting should be creamy but firm enough to hold its shape.

2 Using a pastry bag fitted with a metal tip, pipe frosting onto the cooled cupcakes, using a circular motion.

PER SERVING: 102 calories, 3 g fat (1 g saturated), 1 g protein, 1 g fiber, 17 g sugars, 61 mg sodium, 20 g carbohydrates

port-soaked cherry and dark chocolate brownies

IF THERE'S ONE RECIPE IN THIS chocolate chapter you must try, it has to be these brownies! With the combined decadence of dark chocolate and port-soaked cherries, you can't go wrong with this sexy, smashing hit.

FWB: Cherries

Makes 20

1½ cups fresh cherries, pitted and coarsely chopped

1 cup dried sweet cherries

2 cups sweet port wine (red)

⅓ cup unsalted butter, at room temperature

2 large eggs, lightly beaten

1 tablespoon vanilla extract

⅔ cup all-purpose flour

½ teaspoon baking soda

1 cup sugar

⅔ cup high-quality unsweetened cocoa powder

½ cup buttermilk or sour cream

1½ cups chopped premium dark chocolate

Save the reserved cherry liquid and reduce it in a medium saucepan over low heat. The sauce will thicken and become a sweet cherry–port reduction that you can pour over brownies, frozen yogurt, Cherry-Pistachio Clafoutis (page 215), or anything you please!

1 Completely cover and soak the fresh and dried cherries in the port wine for at least 3 hours (overnight is best). Drain and reserve liquid.

2 Preheat the oven to 350°F. Line the bottom of a 9-inch × 9-inch baking pan with parchment paper and coat it with cooking spray.

3 Melt the chocolate with the butter in a microwave or double boiler. Remove from heat and cool slightly. Add the eggs and vanilla. Whisk until smooth.

4 In a separate bowl, combine the flour, baking soda, sugar, cocoa powder, and dark chocolate. Slowly add the dry ingredients into the melted chocolate mixture, alternating with the buttermilk, stirring to incorporate after each addition. Mix until the batter is smooth and there are no lumps.

5 Gently fold in the port-soaked cherries, reserving a few to garnish and reserving any leftover liquid for another use. Stir to incorporate.

6 Pour the batter into the pan. Bake 40 minutes, or until a toothpick inserted in the center comes out clean. Serve garnished with the reserved cherries.

PER SERVING: 172 calories, 7 g fat (4 g saturated), 3 g protein, 2 g fiber, 17 g sugars, 42 mg sodium, 24 g carbohydrates

chocolate-pistachio soufflé

IF YOU CAN MIX AND WHISK, you can pull these off. Be sure to serve à la minute fresh out of the oven.

FWB: Chocolate, pistachios

Makes 6 servings

3 tablespoons butter, at room temperature

2 tablespoons high-quality unsweetened cocoa powder

1 cup finely chopped premium dark chocolate

2 large egg yolks, at room temperature

1 whole egg, at room temperature

6 large egg whites, at room temperature

⅛ teaspoon sea salt

⅓ cup granulated sugar

¼ cup shelled and finely ground pistachios

Cocoa powder for dusting the soufflés (optional)

1 Preheat the oven to 375°F. Butter 6 ramekins and dust them with the cocoa powder. Set aside.

2 Make a double boiler: Over medium heat, bring a small saucepan halfway filled with water to a simmer. Place a heatproof bowl on top. Reduce the heat to low and melt the chocolate pieces, stirring constantly.

3 Once the chocolate is melted, remove the bowl from the heat and allow it to cool slightly. In a small bowl, beat the egg yolks and whole egg together. To the chocolate, slowly add in the beaten eggs. (Be sure the chocolate isn't too hot, or it will scramble your eggs!)

4 In a separate bowl, using an electric mixer, beat the egg whites with the sea salt on medium-high speed until they hold soft, glossy peaks. Continue beating the egg whites on high speed, gradually adding the sugar, until they hold stiff peaks.

5 Gently stir one-third of the egg whites into the chocolate mixture, then carefully fold in the remaining egg whites. Gently fold in the pistachios until thoroughly combined. The chocolate mixture should be light, bubbly, and evenly colored.

6 Spoon the soufflé mixture into the ramekins, and bake for 15 to 20 minutes, or until they have risen and have a crusty exterior. Dust with cocoa, if desired.

PER SERVING: 350 calories, 24 g fat (13 g saturated), 9 g protein, 3 g fiber, 26 g sugars, 159 mg sodium, 32 g carbohydrates

simple dark chocolate truffles

DREAMY, DECADENT, AND IMPOSSIBLY EASY TO make, these bite-size treats are perfect for any occasion. Try whipping up a batch for your next party. Or pack them in pretty paper liners in to-go boxes as gifts.

FWB: Dark chocolate

Makes 2 dozen

TRUFFLES

3 cups premium semisweet or dark chocolate chips

1 (14-ounce) can sweetened condensed milk

1 tablespoon almond extract (optional)

OPTIONAL TOPPINGS I LOVE

½ cup crushed pistachios

½ cup Lavender Rose Petal Sugar (page 32)

½ cup sweetened shredded coconut

¼ cup high-quality unsweetened dark cocoa powder

¼ cup cinnamon sugar

½ cup crushed peppermint candy canes, for the holidays

1 In a large saucepan, over very low heat, melt the chocolate chips with the sweetened condensed milk. Mix well with a spatula to combine.

2 Remove from the heat and stir in the almond extract, if using.

3 Place the chocolate mixture in a parchment paper–lined loaf pan or shallow bowl and cool completely to room temperature.

4 Using a small melon baller, scoop out the truffle mixture and mold into 1-inch balls. If you don't have a melon baller, use your hands.*

5 To coat the truffles, fill small bowls with toppings, and then roll the truffles in the toppings to coat.

6 Transfer the truffles to paper cupcake liners and refrigerate until ready to serve.

Note that the truffle won't be as smooth.

PER SERVING (1 TRUFFLE): 162 calories, 8 g fat (5 g saturated), 2 g protein, 1 g fiber, 21 g sugars, 24 mg sodium, 24 g carbohydrates

— acknowledgments —

This cookbook was a collaborative effort between many professionals, friends, and colleagues. A heartfelt and huge thanks to . . .

Mom: I am *so* blessed to have been raised by someone so incredibly talented, crafty, intelligent, beautiful, spiritual, and—my goodness—hilarious. Thank you for teaching me about all things food and my deep-rooted Japanese heritage. You are my life sensei. I love you from the depths of my soul. You are my best friend, Mom.

Dad: You are the rock that binds our family. You never let me be anything less than the best. Thank you for raising Jenni and me with integrity, faith, and courage. Your strength, hard work, and refusal to fail at anything shine through us. I love you.

Jenni, my big sis, my philosophical soul mate: Where would I be without your guidance? You are patient, kind, calm, strong, beautiful, talented, and so intelligent. I'd like to say that you and I are living proof that you can live out your dreams. Let's stay allergic to failure forever. I love you, Jen. Go London Bike Kitchen!

David Zinczenko: Thank you for creating opportunities. Your humble guidance is genuinely enriching and your positive motivation infectious. In a very ordinary world, thanks for being such a badass.

Stephen Perrine, the best-dressed man at Rodale: Thank you for being such a positive influence from day one. The expertise and confidence that you have shared with me and in producing this book is beyond appreciated.

Ursula Cary, my amazingly talented editor: I couldn't imagine choosing a better, more intelligent, or more beautiful editor to work with. From the bottom of my heart, thank you.

George Karabotsos, you are such a wonderful spirit. Thank you for your talents with the aesthetic direction for the book cover. I love working with you, you gluten-free gem!

Kara Plikaitis: You are so incredibly talented and the absolute *ichiban* at what you do!

235

Here's to our second beautiful collaboration of many. I'm forever a fan of your work.

Natasha Louise King, my dear friend and art director: For over 4 years we've worked together on some absolutely stunning projects. Thank you for your incredible hard work on every perfect linen, spoon, bit of wallpaper, bowl, cup, insight, and imagination. Your level of taste is exquisite. A big thank you to Tricia Joyce, too!

Lauren Volo: Thank you for such incredibly beautiful food and lifestyle images. The photography in this book tells a story. The images are so stunning, they often had me speechless.

Anna Helm (Charlie's mom): Your food styling and talents shine through your work. Thank you for the long hours and for the massive preproduction days of shopping, baking, testing, etc. I'm so grateful we had the opportunity to work together again!

Alix Winsby: You are such a hard worker, and you did an incredible job prop-styling. I am so grateful for having you on set! You made me smile every day.

William Waldron: Thank you for capturing such an amazing cover shot. You have a way of getting the best from me. Thank you to Martha at True!

For my Stephanie, my best friend, my partner in crime: No matter how far apart we are, you are always close to my heart. I miss you every day! Meredith: Thank you for being my rock and my stylist here in NYC. You've not only tried every tested recipe in this book, you've also seen all the failures. Much like our lives, we've experienced it all together.

To my very best girls in Cali: Andy, Christina, Tina, Suzanne, Casey, Courts, Tanis, Becca, Chrystal, Michelle, Shannon, Angela B.; and in Hawaii, my sisters, Kelly and Dana. You are all with me, in my heart. Molly, Cristina, Allison, Jenelle, Kat, Susan, and Rico: You are my sunshine in NYC. This book is for *all* of you beautiful girls! My DJ Martinez: Without you, travel is not possible. Keep shining, babe.

For all my family, my Baachan in Japan, the Gwiazdowskis, Kumais, Uncle John, Aunt Sally, my Irene, all my little cuzzies in Connecticut, Alicja, Artur, Adam, Aimee, Rose, Joe, DeDe, and the Kryszczynskis: Thank you for the unconditional support and love. Hawaii *ohana*, I love you all, *aloha!*

For Christina Malanga: Thank you for all of your hard work—you make me smile. Carly, thank you for always staying so positive. Janine and Brooks: Thank you for all of your incredible hard work on edits and fact-checks. Without you I could not have written such a solid manuscript. My darling publicist, Danielle Sarna: For taking such good care of me, thank you! Jenelle and Dustin of The Connective, thank you. Emma, you are a very special young lady! For Seevon and Gloria, thank you for making me feel beautiful. For Robert, Leslie, and Mune: Thank you for making me feel gorgeous. For the amazing crew during our shoot, thank you to Molly Schuster, Mister Brett, Jess, Yvette, Stephanie, Matt, Thea, Soo, Janice, Adrianna, Chelsea, Elena, Theeeeo and Cara at BrooklynPhoto studio, a huge hug, green tea, and love!

My dream team at WME: Kirby, Justin, Sherman, Bider, Wachs, Shahkhalili, Conover, Googel, Rosen, Simone, Bethany, Jenni: Thank you for being my strength through the hardest of times. I love you all.

To the team at Rodale Books, *Men's Health*, and *Women's Health*: Maria Rodale, Michele Promaulayko, Bill Phillips, Paul Kita, Hope Clarke, JoAnn Brader, Marie Crousillat, Elizabeth Narins, Jay Ehrlich, Susan Rinkunas, and Michelle Segall-Rainey, thank you! I am so honored to be with such an incredible publisher. To the lovely Aly Mostel and Yelena Nesbit, thank you for your incredible hard work, from *Pretty Delicious* to *Cook Yourself Sexy*!

To my friends at StyleMint, Rebecca Taylor, Joie, Current Elliot, Element, Vans, Lovemarks, Elie Tahari, and Milly, thank you for dressing me! To Kendra Scott Jewels, OliveYew Jewels, and BestNameNecklace, thank you for making me bling, bling. Thank you to the ladies of Bar Method SoHo and San Diego for keeping me fit and disciplined! For Fred DeVito of Exhale Spa, *Namaste*.

For all of my amazing support from my favorite real California farmers: Stan and Derek Azevedo! And for the Chef's Garden in Milan, Ohio. Thank you, Farmer Lee Jones, Mary Jones, and Miss Carrie for the generous and beautiful produce. Kris Moon and the James Beard Foundation, thank you for your support.

For Bob's Red Mill, Woodbridge, POM, Hunter, Eggland's Best, Country Choice oats, Kobrand, Nike, Sugar in the Raw, Pure Dark Chocolate, Justin's Glad, Cake Vintage, Laura Ashley, OXO, Coyne, a huge and heartfelt thank you! I'm grateful that you have shared your high-quality goods with me.

And for all of my prayers answered and my big dreams that have come to pass, my biggest thanks goes to the Good Lord, for you humble me each day. Thank you for my incredible blessings, and I will always continue your good work.

All the faith in the world,
XOX Candice

Foods with Benefits

The following list of my favorite

Foods with Benefits is a great reference for learning more about what each food can offer you. I try to incorporate at least one FWB into every meal of the day. It's easy once you get the hang of it; and your strong, healthy, lean body will thank you! (Please consult your doctor before starting any new health program or with any questions regarding a change in your diet.)

FWB	KEY NUTRIENTS	BENEFITS
Fabulous Fruits		
Apples	Dietary fiber, vitamin C, antioxidants	Healthy heart, promote cardiovascular health; aid digestion
Apricots	Beta-carotene, potassium, antioxidants, vitamin A	Lower blood pressure; help reduce risk of osteoporosis; promote healthy skin, hair, eyes; healthy heart
Avocados	Vitamins A, C, E; monounsaturated good fats	Promote beautiful skin, hair, nails
Bananas	Potassium; folate; vitamins C, B_6, B_1, B_3, K	Help maintain alkali balance; contain good bacteria for healthy tummy!
Cherries	Vitamin C, antioxidants, quercetin, anthocyanins, boron	Anticarcinogenic, anti-inflammatory properties; healthy heart; boost bone health
Dates	Soluble fiber, manganese	Lower cholesterol; boost digestive health, bone health, brain function
Figs	Potassium, calcium, dietary fiber, iron	Lower blood pressure; boost digestive health, bone health
Grapes/Raisins	Antioxidants; potassium; manganese; vitamins C, K	Healthy heart; increase insulin effectiveness; help prevent cancer
Honeydew	Potassium, vitamin C	Boosts immune system; promotes healthy skin; lowers blood pressure
Lemon	Vitamin C, fiber, calcium, iron	Top immunity booster: helps prevent heart disease and cancer
Mango	Vitamins A, C	Promotes beautiful eyes, skin; boosts bone health, immune system
Nectarines	Beta-carotene, vitamin C, potassium, fiber	Promote vibrant eyes, healthy joints (phytochemicals)
Oranges	Vitamins A, B_1, C; folate; potassium; fiber	Help lower blood pressure; have anti-inflammatory properties; boost immune system; help prevent cancer
Peaches	Beta-carotene, vitamin C, potassium, fiber	Promote healthy immune system, vibrant eyes
Pomegranate	Vitamin C, potassium, fiber, antioxidants	Supports healthy immune system, aids digestive health; helps prevent heart disease, cancer

FWB	KEY NUTRIENTS	BENEFITS
Babelicious Berries		
Blueberries	Vitamin C, antioxidants	Promote vibrant eyes, skin; boost brain function; help prevent cancer
Cranberries	Vitamins C, K; fiber	Promote beautiful eyes (major antioxidants)
Raspberries	Vitamin C, antioxidants, calcium, folate	Great for liver, blood; promote vibrant eyes, skin; aid muscle development
Strawberries	Vitamin C, antioxidants	Promote vibrant eyes, skin; lower blood cholesterol; help prevent cancer
Vibrant Veggies		
Artichoke	Fiber; calcium; iron; vitamins C, B_1, B_2, B_3, B_6	Stabilizes blood sugar; natural diuretic; helps protect that liver!
Asparagus	Fiber; manganese; vitamins A, C, K, B_1, B_3, B_6	Healthy heart; boosts kidney, lung health; promotes gorgeous eyes; natural diuretic; helps prevent cancer
Beets	Folate, fiber, iron, vitamin C, antioxidants	Decrease risk of coronary artery disease; may reduce risk of brain or spinal cord birth defects; low in calories
Bok choy	Potassium, calcium, vitamin D	Strengthens teeth, bones; helps balance natural electrolytes
Brussels sprouts	Vitamins A, B_6, C, K; manganese; folate; fiber; omega-3 (ALA)	Help prevent breast, cervical, ovarian, prostate cancers; anti-inflammatory properties; aid digestive health
Butternut squash	Vitamins A, B_6, C; fiber; potassium; folate	Anti-inflammatory properties; provides essential nutrients for fetal development; healthy heart; promotes digestive health; helps prevent breast cancer
Cabbage	Fiber; folate; vitamins B_6, C, K	Totally detoxifies the body naturally; aids digestive health; natural diuretic; promotes women's overall health
Carrots	Beta-carotene; vitamins A, C, K	Promote superhealthy eyes; help prevent cancer, heart disease; help regulate blood sugar
Cauliflower	Vitamins B_5, B_6, C, K; folate; potassium	Helps prevent breast, cervical, ovarian, prostate cancers; anti-inflammatory properties; aids digestive health
Cucumber	Vitamins A, C; fiber; silica	Promotes radiant skin; helps lower high blood pressure

FWB	KEY NUTRIENTS	BENEFITS
Daikon radish	Anthoxanthin, vitamin C	Natural diuretic; aids digestion, detoxification
Eggplant	Potassium; fiber; vitamins B_1, B_6, B_3	Boosts brain function, cardiovascular health, immunity; natural diuretic
Fennel	Fiber, potassium, vitamin C	Fat and cholesterol free! Helps maintain healthy blood pressure (low in sodium)
Garlic	Manganese; vitamins B_6, C	Antioxidant; antibacterial properties; helps regulate blood sugar; boosts bone health
Gobo root aka Burdock root	Inulin, potassium, iron, manganese, magnesium	Fat free, saturated fat free, cholesterol free, and sodium free! Antioxidant; helps control heart rate, blood pressure; helps reduce blood sugar, cholesterol levels
Green onion	Calcium; vitamins A, B_1, C	Helps lower blood sugar, cholesterol; helps prevent cancer; helps reduce inflammation
Kabocha	Vitamins A, C; beta-carotene; iron; potassium	Promotes beautiful, healthy eyes; helps maintain moisture in skin; helps lower LDL cholesterol, blood pressure; boosts bone health
Onions	Fiber, vitamin C	Antibacterial properties; strengthen bones; aid digestion, help prevent cancer
Parsnips	Fiber, potassium, vitamin C	Decrease risk of coronary heart disease; maintain healthy blood pressure; low in calories
Potatoes	Fiber; folate; calcium; iron; vitamins C, B_6, B_1, B_3, K, E	Help maintain fluid balance, regulate blood pressure; healthy heart; promote healthy, sexy brain!
Pumpkin	Potassium; fiber; vitamins A, C, B_6, B_3, B_5	Promotes healthy lungs, beautiful eyes; helps maintain moisture in skin
Red bell peppers	Fiber; vitamins A, C, K, B_6	Promote healthy lungs, cardiovascular health, beautiful eyes
Sweet potatoes	Iron; vitamins A, C; fiber	Promote gorgeous skin; boost immunity; great for blood circulation
Tomatoes	Lycopene	Promote vibrant eyes; help prevent prostate cancer
Turnips	Fiber, calcium, vitamin C	Decrease risk of coronary artery disease; promote healthy teeth, gums; protect against infections; low in calories

FWB	KEY NUTRIENTS	BENEFITS
Zucchini	Fiber; potassium; manganese; vitamins A, C	Anti-inflammatory properties; aids digestion; helps keep you fuller longer (high water content); low in calories

Squash blossoms are also a great pick!

Dark & Mysterious Leafy Greens

FWB	KEY NUTRIENTS	BENEFITS
Arugula	Vitamins A, C; folate; magnesium	Aphrodisiac; keeps eyes bright; promotes overall optimum health
Kale	Vitamins A, B_6, C, K; manganese; fiber; omega-3s	Helps prevent cancer; improves blood clotting; anti-inflammatory properties; promotes cardiovascular health
Mustard greens/Collards/Mizuna	Folate; vitamins A, C, K; fiber	Overall superfoods for optimal, sexy health—promote bright eyes, vibrant skin, healthy lungs
Romaine	Vitamins A, C, K; antioxidants	Promotes bright eyes, healthy heart; aids digestion
Spinach	Vitamins A, C, K, B_2, B_6, B_1; iron; folate	Popeye was no joke—keeps you strong! Total supersexy food—promotes strong bones, healthy heart; helps prevent cancer
Swiss chard	Potassium; iron; fiber; vitamins A, C, E, K	Promotes beautiful eyes, gorgeous clear skin
Watercress	Vitamins C, E, K; beta-carotene; antioxidants	Promotes healthy, clear skin

Healing + Happy Herbs

FWB	KEY NUTRIENTS	BENEFITS
Basil	Vitamins A, K; iron; flavanoids	Great for cardiovascular health; antibiotic; anti-inflammatory properties; aids digestion; helps relieve tummy aches
Cilantro	Fiber, manganese, iron, flavanoids	Aids digestion; prevents nausea; relieves intestinal gas (wow!); lowers blood sugar levels, cholesterol
Mint	Vitamins A, C	Soothes upset stomach, irritable bowel
Oregano	Vitamin K, manganese, iron, antioxidants	Antibacterial properties; promotes bone health, blood clotting
Parsley	Vitamins A, C, K; folate; iron; major antioxidants	Major supersexy food—healthy heart; freshens breath; aids digestion; strong diuretic
Sage	Vitamin K	Helps relieve hot flashes and other menopausal symptoms; antiseptic properties

FWB	KEY NUTRIENTS	BENEFITS
Thyme	Vitamin K, iron, manganese, calcium	Essential for normal blood clotting; antimicrobial properties; promotes bone health

Meaty Mushrooms

Cremini mushrooms	Selenium; zinc; vitamins B_1, B_2, B_6, B_3	Boost immunity, energy; may help prevent Alzheimer's; help lower cholesterol
Shiitake mushrooms	Iron, protein, fiber, vitamin C	Boost immunity; promote optimal health; may help lower cholesterol

The Seedy Side of Life: Grains/Seeds

Barley	Fiber, selenium, tryptophan	Boosts immunity; aids digestion; helps prevent cancer
Bran	Protein, iron, fiber	Minimizes risk of diabetes, aids digestion (yes, it does!); lowers cholesterol; natural probiotic
Brown rice	Fiber, protein, manganese, selenium	Aids digestion
Flaxseed	Omega-3s, monounsaturated good fat, protein, fiber	Boosts brain health; promotes beautiful hair, skin, nails; aids digestion; helps keep skin moisturized, supple
Oats	Fiber, protein, manganese, selenium	Help lower cholesterol, blood pressure; promote optimum function of kidneys, liver, spleen; protect against diabetes, heart disease
Pumpkin seeds	Manganese, magnesium, protein, zinc	Promote prostate, bone health; have anti-inflammatory properties; healthy heart
Quinoa	Fiber, complete protein, manganese, magnesium, iron	Aids cardiovascular health, digestion; prevents migraines; helps prevent heart disease, cancer; lowers type 2 diabetes risk
Spelt	Manganese, fiber, protein	Healthy heart; lowers cholesterol; helps prevent breast cancer, gallstones

Magic Beans

Black beans	Vitamin B_1, protein, fiber, folate	Help lower high blood pressure; aid digestion; pack on energy
Edamame/Soy	Fiber; protein; vitamins A, C; calcium; iron	Helps prevent cancer, lower cholesterol; boosts immune system
Garbanzo beans/ Chickpeas	Fiber, protein, folate, manganese	Help lower cholesterol (great source), stabilize blood sugar levels; aid digestion; healthy heart

FWB	KEY NUTRIENTS	BENEFITS
Green beans	Vitamins A, C, K; potassium; fiber	Lower blood pressure; keep bones healthy; aid cardiovascular health
Kidney beans	Fiber, protein, folate, manganese	Aid digestion; help lower cholesterol, stabilize blood sugar levels
Lentils	Folate, fiber, iron, protein	Aid digestion; healthy heart; great for weight loss

Nutzo for Nuts

Almonds	Vitamin E, manganese, selenium	Help lower risk of heart disease; may help lower cholesterol; help keep skin moisturized, supple, glowing
Hazelnuts	Vitamin E, copper, manganese, folate	Help keep skin moisturized, supple, glowing; healthy heart; may reduce risk of urinary tract infections; decrease risk of birth defects
Peanut butter	Protein, fiber, good fats, vitamin E, resveratrol	Healthy lean plant protein
Pistachios	Fiber, B vitamins, thiamine, copper	Healthy heart; great for weight loss!
Walnuts	Good fats, omega-3s	Boost brain health; healthy heart; minimize premature aging and wrinkles; boost mood; decrease appetite

Fins 'n' Shells

Clams	Omega-3s, protein, iron, selenium	Nutrient-dense iron powerhouse; healthy heart
Crab	Protein, vitamin B_{12}, zinc, omega-3s	Lowers stress levels; anti-inflammatory properties; healthy heart
Mahi mahi	Vitamin A, protein, iron	Keeps you lean and mean; promotes healthy skin, bright eyes
Pacific cod	Protein; omega-3s; vitamins B_3, B_6, B_{12}; potassium	Lowers blood pressure; promotes healthy fetal development; boosts brain function; anti-inflammatory properties
Pacific sardines	Protein; omega-3s; vitamins B_{12}, D; calcium	Lower blood pressure; promote healthy fetal development; boost brain function; anti-inflammatory properties
Salmon	Omega-3s, monounsaturated fats, fiber	Improves circulation; promotes shiny hair and gorgeous, bright, beautiful skin; boosts brain health

FWB	KEY NUTRIENTS	BENEFITS
Scallops	Omega-3s, protein, vitamin B_{12}, selenium	Healthy heart; help prevent cancer; decrease risk of stroke; boost brain function
Shrimp	Protein; vitamins D, B_{12}; selenium; iron	May prevent against Alzheimer's; improve mood; helps prevent and control high blood pressure
Trout	Protein; omega-3s; niacin; vitamins B_6, B_{12}	Lowers blood pressure; promotes healthy fetal development; boosts brain function; anti-inflammatory properties
Tuna	Protein, vitamin A, omega-3s	Boosts sexy brain health; lowers blood pressure, cholesterol; promotes healthy skin

Lean Machine

FWB	KEY NUTRIENTS	BENEFITS
Chicken breast (try to purchase organic, free range)*	Vitamin B_3, B_6; lean protein	Keeps you lean and mean; promotes healthy, glowing skin; strengthens bones; boosts energy
Lean beef (try to purchase grass fed, free farmed)*	Lean protein; amino acids; vitamins B_2, B_3, B_6, B_{12}; zinc; iron	Aids emotional and mental well being, cardiovascular health; boosts brain health, red blood cells, energy
Lean deli meats*	Lean protein, essential amino acids, collagen	Keeps you lean and mean; promotes healthy, glowing skin
Tofu!	Protein, antioxidants, omega-3s	Lean protein source
Pork	Vitamins B_6, B_{12}; niacin; riboflavin; thiamine	Helps maintain healthy metabolism; promotes healthy immune system
Eggs	Protein; vitamins A, D, B_6, B_{12}; folate; choline	Lean protein source; anti-inflammatory properties; promote healthy eyes; boost brain function

Nondairy/Cheeses

FWB	KEY NUTRIENTS	BENEFITS
Almond milk	Vitamins D, E; iron; phosphorus; calcium	Promotes beautiful hair, skin, nails; easily digested; low in calories; supercreamy, delicious nondairy alternative to milk!
Chèvre (goat cheese)	Calcium, protein	Easier to digest than cow's milk; promotes totally gorgeous hair, skin, nails
Greek yogurt	Protein, calcium, vitamin D	Promotes totally gorgeous hair, skin, nails; strong bones; flat belly
Parmesan cheese*	Calcium, protein	Promotes sexy hair, nails, skin, teeth

*Eat in moderation

FWB	KEY NUTRIENTS	BENEFITS
Spicy Sexy		
Cinnamon	Manganese, fiber, iron, calcium	The scent alone may boost cognitive function and memory! Improves colon health; antiseptic properties; aids digestion; benefits heart, lungs, kidneys
Coriander	Iron, manganese, magnesium, fiber	Aids intestinal health; helps relieve intestinal gas (fabulous!); protects against urinary tract infections; helps lower bad cholesterol
Cumin	Iron, manganese	Helps boost immunity, energy; helps prevent cancer; promotes prenatal, blood health
Curry powder	Vitamins B_6, E; calcium; iron; zinc	Promotes healthy joints; helps prevent Alzheimer's by improving memory; has anti-inflammatory properties
Ginger	Antioxidants	Anti-inflammatory properties; helps alleviate morning sickness; may relieve motion sickness
Nutmeg	Iron, calcium	Increases blood circulation; anti-inflammatory properties; may help curb appetite
Bonus!		
Extra-virgin olive oil	Monounsaturated good fat	Biggest supersexy food of them all! Beauty in a bottle for healthy hair, skin, nails; healthy heart; may help with longevity; protects against heart disease; helps lower cholesterol
Honey	Antioxidants	May help alleviate seasonal allergy symptoms; antibacterial properties; suppresses coughs; promotes beautiful, supple skin
Soba	Protein, iron, fiber	Helps lower cholesterol; lowers blood pressure; aids digestion; great gluten-free alternative to wheat pasta
Whole wheat bread*	Protein, iron, fiber	Keeps you fuller longer; aids digestion
Antioxidant Heaven		
Cocoa powder / Chocolate*	Antioxidants, flavanoids	Promotes cardiovascular health; may aid in anti-aging; healthy heart; um, and it's absolutely delish!
Red vino!**	Antioxidants, flavanoids, reservatol	May aid in anti-aging! healthy heart; helps protect lining of heart

*Eat in moderation **Drink in moderation

— index —